OBSERVATIONS ON \

VOL. 2

PRICE - TIME - VOLUME - VELOCITY

OBSERVATIONS ON W.D. GANN

VOL. 2

PRICE - TIME - VOLUME - VELOCITY

AWODELE

BEKH

UNION, KY ™

BEKH, LLC
UNION, KY
BEKHLLC@OUTLOOK.COM

ISBN-10: 0692666524
ISBN-13: 978-0692666524

TABLE OF CONTENTS

PREFACE

It was in February of 1997 when I met my most influential spiritual teacher. A friend took me to see him for the first time during one of my breaks from classes. On the first visit he divined for me using an oracle system, performed a numerology reading on my date of birth, and told me things about myself that were quite astonishing considering that this was the first time we had ever met. I was fascinated and it sealed a friendship that has lasted ever since.

During the remaining part of 1997, which included my senior year of college and the start of graduate school, I would continue to go to his office to visit. He would always pass along books, notes, and material that he had picked up along the way to see if I resonated with any of the information. I loved it all, but will never forget the document he gave me with the title *Spiritual Development* written at the top. It was a copy of some handwritten notes dated November 2, 1975. There was no mention of the lecturer's name, but more importantly, the subject matter stimulated me like nothing else had before. I was captivated. The main theme of the lecture dealt with cycles and the advantage one can gain by living in harmony with them. It talked about how the sages used cycles for spiritual, mental, and physical development. This lit an inner fire in me to learn as much about cycles as I could.

As my interest and study of cycles grew, I obtained my first book on astrology during this time. Although this first book was on Vedic Astrology, I have studied many forms of astrology over the years. Naturally, studying subjects such as cycles and astrology, I eventually came across the work of W.D. Gann.

William Delbert Gann was born on June 6, 1878 in Lufkin, Texas. In his promotional booklet issued in 1954, it says that he made his first trade in commodities on August 15, 1902, but his fame spread as a result of the December 1909 *Ticker and Investment Digest* magazine article written by R.D. Wyckoff, who was owner of the magazine at that time. In this article, Gann talked about "The Law of Vibration", and how it enabled him to accurately predict the points at which stocks would rise and fall. Numerous examples are given in the article where Gann predicts that a stock would not go higher or lower than a certain price. It goes on to say that in the presence of a representative of the *Ticker and Investment Digest* during the month of October 1909, Gann made 286 transactions in various stocks during 25 market days and that 240 of the 286 transactions were profitable. It said that the capital with which he operated was doubled ten times so that at the end of the month he had 1,000 percent of his original margin.

In Gann's promotional booklet entitled, *Why Money is Lost on Commodities and Stocks and How to Make Profits from 1954*, it records the following:

"1908 May 12th left Oklahoma City for New York City. August 8th made one of his greatest mathematical discoveries for predicting the trend of stocks and commodities. Started trading with a capital of $300 and made $25,000. Started another account with $130 and made $12,000 in thirty days time."

Here we have an individual that could forecast the movement of stocks months and years in advance, and his ability to do so was well documented. After reading more about him and his work, I was intrigued, and set out to learn as much as I could.

During my time studying Gann, I was fortunate to come across an e-book published by the Gann Study Group entitled, *W.D. Gann on the Law of Vibration.* In this e-book is where I first read a little known Gann article from 1919. In this article, Gann makes some predictions about the German Kaiser, Wilhelm Hohenzollern, and provides some details as to how he made his predictions. Like the document on *Spiritual Development* in 1997, I was captivated. Continued study and work on the contents of the article led to the publication of my first book in June 2013 entitled, *W.D. Gann: Divination By Mathematics.* Later that year, I published my second book entitled *W.D. Gann: Divination By Mathematics: Harmonic Analysis.*

In that book, the main goal was to decipher what Gann may have meant when he used the words "harmonic analysis" in his novel entitled, *The Tunnel Thru the Air Or Looking Back From 1940.* What seemed to match his reference to these words was the branch of mathematics that I described in *W.D. Gann: Divination By Mathematics: Harmonic Analysis.* In addition, I made an attempt to explain in simple language how to use this math to perform harmonic analysis on a set of data. Interestingly, shortly after the publication of that book, I came across some material I had not seen related to the same subject matter. In addition, there was a connection to Gann, and it seemed to answer some of the questions I had left off with in that publication. Thus, one of the goals of this book is to simply share this additional information along with the ideas that have resulted from its investigation.

It has always been my intention to publish additional books to get some of the ideas that I have been working with out in the open, but I never believed I had enough information on a particular topic to fill a three hundred, two hundred, or even a one hundred page book. With this in mind, I realized that I could publish small booklets in a series of volumes, each focusing on a different topic to achieve my goal. Although the page count for this current volume is much larger than I thought I would be able to produce, this is what you will find in this publication, a small booklet on Price, Time, Volume, and Velocity, which is the second volume in a series of volumes on observations I have made with respect to Gann's work. It is my hope that the reader will find something valuable within these pages to further their own research and study.

Awodele,
Union, KY

March 11, 2016

1

HARMONIC ANALYSIS REVISITED

In Chapter XVI of the novel entitled, *The Tunnel Thru the Air or Looking Back From 1940*, the main character, Robert Gordon, is engaged in a conversation with an older gentleman by the name of Mr. Henry Watson who he is introduced to by his friend Walter Kennelworth. Mr. Watson recounts many stories about individuals who made a success on Wall Street, but only to lose the majority of their profits in the end. Robert then asks Mr. Watson if anyone had ever made a large fortune out of Wall Street and kept it. Mr. Watson replied as follows:

> *"Oh, yes . . . if there were not exceptions to the rule, business would not continue to run. I could tell you of dozens of them, but one striking example is that of the late E. H. Harriman who died worth about three hundred million dollars. He had probably made out of the market a hundred million dollars in the last three or four years of his life. Robert asked, How did he do it? Mr. Watson answered, He stuck to one class of stocks - railroads. He studied them day and night, never diverted his attention*

to other lines. I believe that he possessed some math-ematical method which enabled him to forecast stocks many months and years in advance. I have gone over his manipulations and the stocks he traded in, and found that they conform closely to the law of harmonic analy-sis. He certainly knew something about time and season because he bought at the right time and sold at the right time."

The first thing that stands out when you read this passage is the reference to E. H. Harriman. If you are familiar with the *Ticker and Investment Digest* article from December 1909, then you may already know what I am referring to. In this article, Gann writes as follows with respect to the Law of Vibration:

"In order to test the efficiency of my idea I have not only put in years of labour in the regular way, but I spent nine months working night and day in the Astor Library in New York and in the British Museum of London, go-ing over the records of stock transactions as far back as 1820. I have incidentally examined the manipulations of Jay Gould, Daniel Drew, Commodore Vanderbilt & all other important manipulators from that time to the pres-ent day. I have examined every quotation of Union Pacific prior to & from the time of E. H. Harriman, Mr. Harriman's was the most masterly. The figures show that, whether unconsciously or not, Mr. Harriman worked strictly in ac-cordance with natural law."

It is apparent that Gann thought highly of the manipulations of E. H. Harriman, so much in fact that he would add reference to him in his novel eighteen years after first mentioning him in the December 1909 *Ticker and Investment Digest* article. Not only that, but here we find that Gann is saying that Mr. Harriman worked strictly in accordance with natural law. Why is this important? In the very same article, Gann says as follows:

> *"I soon began to note the periodical recurrence of the rise and fall in stocks and commodities. This led me to conclude that natural law was the basis of market movements."*

Gann is saying that he believes natural law to be the basis of market movements and that E. H. Harriman worked in strict accordance with this law. Furthermore, we have additional information from page 205 of Gann's novel as to what this may be. It is on page 205 where Mr. Watson says that he believed E. H. Harriman possessed some "mathematical method," which enabled him to forecast stocks many months and years in advance, and that his manipulations conformed closely to the law of harmonic analysis. Naturally, I wanted to know more about this mathematical method, and thought that it would be related to Gann's reference to the "law of harmonic analysis".

When I typed in "Law of Harmonic Analysis" in the internet search engine, it returned less than ten results, and the majority of those came from Gann's novel. However, when I typed in "Harmonic Analysis", it returned a number of pages. One was a Wikipedia entry that read as follows:

"Harmonic analysis is a branch of mathematics concerned with the representation of functions or signals as the superposition of basic waves, and the study of and generalization of the notions of Fourier series and Fourier transforms."

I was excited to hear that it was referring to a branch of mathematics since Gann's novel indicated that E.H. Harriman's possessed some "mathematical method". Wanting to find out more about this, I looked up Fourier series and found the following, which is also from Wikipedia.

"In mathematics, a Fourier series decomposes periodic functions or periodic signals into the sum of a (possibly infinite) set of simple oscillating functions, namely sines and cosines (or complex exponentials). . . The Fourier series is named in honour of Jean-Baptiste Joseph Fourier (1768-1830), who made important contributions to the study of trigonometric series, after preliminary investigations by Leonhard Euler, Jean le Rond d'Alembert, and Daniel Bernoulli. . . Fourier introduced the series for the purpose of solving the heat equation in a metal plate, publishing his initial results in his 1807 Memoire sur la propagation de le chaleur dans les corps solides (Treatise on the propagation of heat in solid bodies), and publishing his Theorie analytique de la chaleur in 1822. Early ideas of decomposing a periodic function into the sum of simple oscillating functions date back to the 3rd century BC, when ancient astronomers proposed an empiric model of planetary motions, based on deferents and epicycles."

Afterwards, I looked up Jean-Baptiste Joseph Fourier and found that he was a French mathematician and physicist and was best known for initiating the investigation of Fourier series and their applications to problems of heat transfer and vibrations. This, and the description of Fourier series tied a lot of things together for me. When you consider the fact that Gann said himself that he used mathematics to forecast markets, and the fact that we have the passage from the novel were Gann is making a reference to a branch of mathematics that deals with vibration analysis, it is hard to look away from this.

Furthermore, when you consider what Gann said in the 1919 *Milwaukee Sentinel Magazine* article, that he made his discovery about twenty years ago, after weeks and months of research into geometry and mathematics in ancient books, and the fact that early ideas of decomposing a periodic function into the sum of simple oscillating functions date back to the 3rd century BC when ancient astronomers proposed an empiric model of planetary motions based on deferents and epicycles, it is even harder to look away. In the 1919 article Gann stated,

> *"An astronomer can predict to the minute when an eclipse is going to occur . . . but you would not consider him a prophet, would you? Of course not, He simply makes use of mathematics based on known laws of the movements of the planets in their orbits. . . I use geometry and mathematics just as an astronomer does, based on immutable laws which I have discovered."*

That said, I suspected that Harmonic Analysis may have been used by Gann in his work. There is more evidence in *Tunnel Thru the Air* where the words "harmonic analysis" is used in the only other place in that book. On page 77 in Chapter VII on Future Cycles, the main character, Robert Gordon, writes the following in a letter dated January 28, 1927:

> *"The limit of future predictions based on exact mathematical law is only restricted by lack of knowledge of correct data on past history to work from. . . A few years ago even scientific men, not alone the public, would have laughed at such a thing and refused to believe it. But mathematical science, which is the only real science that the entire civilized world has agreed upon, furnishes unmistakable proof of history repeating itself and shows that the cycle theory, or harmonic analysis, is the only thing that we can rely upon to ascertain the future."*

If you read the above passage carefully, it seems as if he is equating "harmonic analysis" with "the cycle theory". This is important to grasp because on page 75 in the beginning of the chapter, Robert Gordon says,

> *"In making my predictions I use geometry and mathematics, just as the astronomer does, based on immutable laws. . . My calculations are based on the cycle theory and on mathematical sequences."*

Sound familiar? The first part of that passage is a carbon copy of what we found in the 1919 article. If Gann was equating "the cycle theory" with "harmonic analysis" on page 77 of his novel, then couldn't the passage on page 75 also read, "My calculations are based on [harmonic analysis] and on mathematical sequences."

Now, after a closer examination of the e-book entitled, *W.D. Gann on The Law of Vibration*, published by the Gann Study Group, harmonic analysis is associated with the subject of mathematics in a footnote on page 11. It reads as follows:

"HARMONIC ANALYSIS, in mathematics, the name given by Sir William Thomson (Lord Kelvin) and P. G. Tait in their treatise on Natural Philosophy to a general method of investigating physical questions, the earliest applications of which seem to have been suggested by the study of the vibration of strings and the analysis of these vibrations into their fundamental tone and its harmonics or overtones."

Given the information thus far provided, the most simple explanation of harmonic analysis that I came across during my research that helped me to understand what the math was actually doing came from an online article entitled, *An Interactive Guide to the Fourier Transform* by Kalid Azad. It went something like this, imagine that you have a smoothie, and let's say that you don't know all of the ingredients that were blended together to make that smoothie. We can say that Harmonic Analysis will allow you to extract the individual ingredients that were blended together to make the smoothie. In other words, it will enable you to identify what those ingredients are. Now, if you were to recombine the major ingredients that you were able to identify, you would be able to create a smoothie that somewhat looked and tasted like the original.

If you can now think of the price values plotted on a stock chart as representing the smoothie, we can say that its ingredients are composed of a number of periodic cycles of various lengths. Thus, harmonic analysis will enable you to identify the dominant cycles that make up the graph of the value of stock prices over time. The dominant cycles can be identified in the calculated values of the coefficients of the Fourier Series, which can also be graphed to display the most dominant values. Furthermore, through the use of the formula for a Fourier Series, you can take the values of the coefficients representing the most dominant cycles and re-combine them to produce a periodic waveform that mimics the graph of the original data. Not only that, but this formula also allows you to project that curve into the future many months and years.

In my previous publication, *W.D. Gann: Divination By Mathematics: Harmonic Analysis*, I described the procedure utilized by Henry Ludwell Moore in his book entitled, *Economic Cycles: Their Law and Cause*, as an example to show how to perform harmonic analysis on a set of data. If you are interested in this method of analysis, you can refer to my previous publication as I will not revisit it here. However, going forward, I will go over the additional material I learned about shortly after publishing my first book on harmonic analysis. It comes from Professor Weston's booklet entitled, *Forecasting the New York Stock Market*. As I stated, it seemed to answer some of the questions I left off with in my previous publication.

One of these questions came as a result of reading an article from *The (New York) Sun* dated December 28, 1921. In the article, Gann is forecasting what would be in store for 1922. More importantly, the contents of the article contained additional information that harmonic analysis was indeed something that needed to be investigated further. In one part of the article, it reads as follows:

> *"Asked to explain his method of figuring out future events, Mr. Gann refers it all to mathematical law, employed in connection with a close analysis of the past. The idea is that history of the stock market, for instance, or of the cotton market, or the weather, or influenza, or the price of pig iron fluctuates in definite cycles, and if you work out the cyclic periods, and give some intelligent study to operating causes, you can soon win promotion into the prophet class."*

In addition, it reads,

> *"One of his stunts [Gann] is to project a curve for the stock market, showing when it should be prosperous and when depressed. In that operation he uses a system of his own, simplified from that propounded by Henry Ludwell Moore, professor of political economy at Columbia University, in his work, Economic Cycles, Their Law and Cause."*

Out of all the different books and papers that I had come across during my research, this is the one book that I thought would be best for me to learn how to perform harmonic analysis, and here I read about it in an article associated with Mr. Gann. Furthermore, it said that Gann was using a system of his own, but that it was a simplified form of Harmonic Analysis from that described by Moore in his book. This article aroused the first question that I had left off with in my previous publication. How did Gann simplify Henry Ludwell's Moore's approach to harmonic analysis?

At the end of an e-mail that I received, the sender had pointed out that Gann had acknowledged familiarity with Moore's work in another place. It was in a letter dated April 1, 1926 to John H. Spohn, who appears to be one of Gann's clients. This letter, which is part of a series of letters in a document entitled, *Letters by W.D. Gann to John H. Spohn and Dr. John De Jonge*, contains the following statement from Gann.

> *"I have read Professor Moore's book and the trouble with him was that he failed to get the right time factor and of course did not know the cause behind market movements."*

This letter aroused the next two questions that I had left off with in my previous publication. Gann said that Moore failed to get the right time factor, and that he did not know the cause behind market movements. What is the time factor, and what is the cause behind market movements? In my opinion, these questions are our clues as to how Gann may have simplified the method of Moore and how it may have differed from Moore's approach. In my previous publication I addressed the possible cause for cycles from Gann's own writings. One possible cause is the planets.

2

THE CAUSE OF CYCLES

The evidence that planetary cycles may be the cause comes directly from one of Gann's courses. Under a section entitled, "How to Forecast", Gann states as follows:

> "The next important cycle is 30 years, which is caused by the planet Saturn. This planet makes one revolution around the sun every 30 years. Saturn rules the products of the earth and causes extreme high or low prices in products of the earth at the end of each 30-year cycle, and this makes Stocks high or low."

In this passage, he literally tells you that the orbit of Saturn around the sun causes the 30 year cycle. In support of this planetary cause for cycles is Professor Weston's manuscript on *Forecasting the New York Stock Market*.

First and foremost, there is an established connection between Professor Weston and W.D. Gann. Professor Weston is also known as L. H. Weston, who also wrote another book entitled, *The Fixed Stars in Astrology*. In the e-book entitled, *W.D. Gann on the Law of Vibration*, there is an image of the cover of an issue of the *Astrological Bullentina* which contains a list of the zodiac council members for an organization called The Astrological Society, Inc., N. Y. There are many recognizable names such as W. Gorn Old (Sepharial) listed under Pisces, Lyman E. Stowe under Aries, and W. D. Gann under Gemini, but what I would like to point out is that L. H. Weston is listed under Capricorn. Please see the cover on the following page. They were all part of the zodiac council for this organization.

Since we find these individuals all part of the same Astrological Society, I don't think it is farfetched that they shared ideas. That said, Professor Weston's book is also known as the *Weston Papers*, which is a treatise on the Geometrical or Chart System of Forecasting. Now, one of the questions I mentioned before is how did Gann simplify Henry Ludwell's Moore's approach to harmonic analysis? In Professor Weston's book, we find a possible answer as the method described is indeed a much simpler method than that described by Moore.

Moore described a very tedious process by which one identifies the most dominant cycles within a set of data. Weston on the other hand uses what he calls, the cut-and-try method. On page 8 of *Forecasting the New York Stock Market*, he writes,

> *"The highly technical methods of applying periodograms of the amplitude of oscillation for the time units, and testing the deviations from the harmonics by the least squares may all be used if the student cares to take the pains to try them on the Potato curve or any other kind of a curve, but in actual practice the method here recom-*

mended and used is the common old method of "cut-and-try." If the investigator can not find any cycles by the simple cut-and-try plan then it is exceedingly probable he would never find any useful ones by means of the periodograms or least squares. We do not want any cycles unless they are useful ones, and if they are useful they will almost certainly be plain enough in the records to admit of being picked up after a few trials with the cut-and-try plan."

Weston goes on to describe the method by which you look at the maximum points in the graph that you are analyzing and note the distribution of the tops in the general field of vision. He notes that in the Potato curve, which he uses as the example in his book, the tops come out somewhere near 3 years apart. He also says that by drawing a dotted line through in such a way as to represent the general averages in 3-year periods, that there must be a long-swing component of near 20 years. Continuing on page 8 he writes,

"This simple method of mere inspection, keeping in mind our fundamental theories, advances us at once to the point of determining very closely the two principal components of the Potato curve. . . By this very simple, yet strictly mathematical and scientific process we are able to determine very closely the exact length of two harmonics in the Potato curve and fix their epochs, for we see quite plainly that, the cosines in the supposed 20-year cycle must osculate about in December of the years 1881 and 1901."

It is here that I must explain what Weston meant when referencing the cosines before proceeding further in this discourse.

Trigonometry comes from the Greek trigonon, "triangle" and metron, "measure". It is a branch of mathematics that studies the relationships involving lengths and angles of triangles. The field emerged during the 3rd century BC from applications of geometry to astronomical studies. A right angled triangle is a triangle where one of its angles measures 90 degrees. This is pictured below.

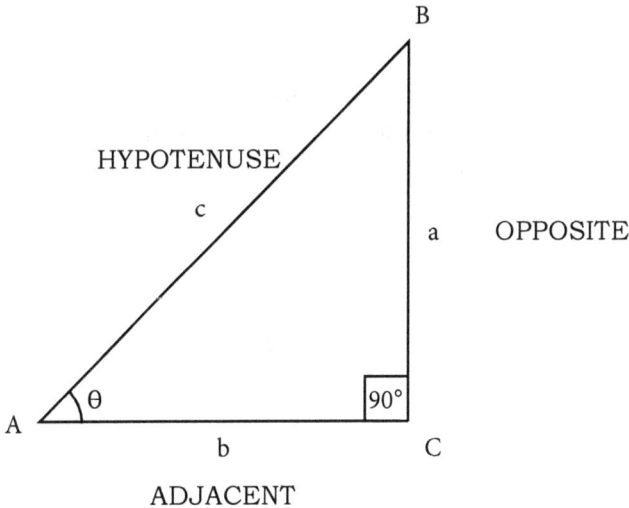

In a right angled triangle, The Greek letter theta "θ" is a label for the angle you are working with. It can never be 90° in the formulas for right angled triangles. The side opposite the 90° angle is labeled the hypotenuse. The side opposite theta "θ" is called the opposite. The side next to theta "θ" is labeled adjacent. The angles are labeled with capital letters

(A,B,C), and the sides with lowercase letters (a,b,c). Note, the sides opposite the angles are labeled with the lowercase letter of the corresponding angle.

"SOHCAHTOA" is a mnemonic for remembering how to compute the sine, cosine, and tangent of an angle. The first part of the mnemonic is SOH, and stands for the formula where the "S" sine of an angle is equal to the "O" opposite side over the "H" hypotenuse. The middle part of the mnemonic is CAH, which stands for the formula where the "C" cosine of an angle is equal to the "A" adjacent side over the "H" hypotenuse. The last part of the mnemonic is TOA, which stands for the formula where the "T" tangent of an angle is equal to the "O" opposite side over the "A" adjacent side.

As an example, let's say we have a 3, 4, 5 right angled triangle as depicted below.

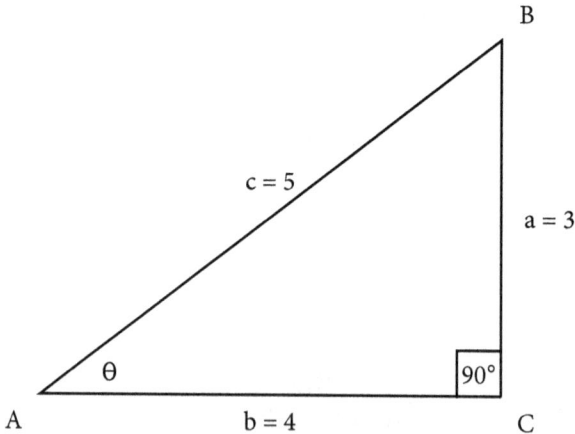

The sine of an angle is the opposite side over the hypotenuse. This would be 3/5, which is .6. To get the angle "θ", we calculate the inverse of the sine value of .6 and get 36.8698

degrees or if working in radians, .6435. Note, 360° is equal to 2 times Pi radians, which is 6.2831853 (2 X 3.14159). If we only have the angle "θ", we can calculate the sine, which gives us the ratio between the opposite side and the hypotenuse. Starting with 36.8698 degrees, we would put this in the calculator and hit the sine key and get .59999 or .6 rounded up. The sine and cosine of an angle will always be a number between -1 and 1. Now lets add a circle to the image to get a better understanding of what is taking place.

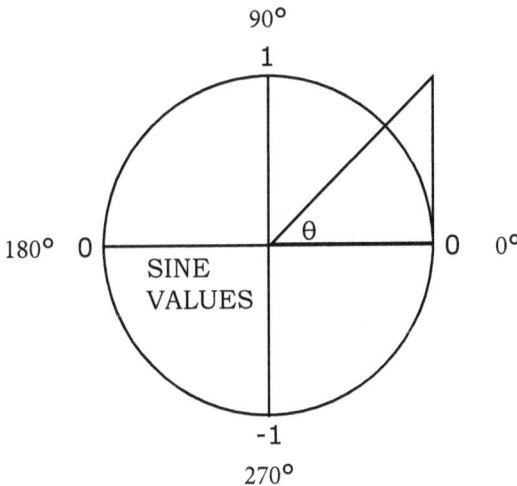

The sine of an angle of 0° is zcro. As you go around the circle, the sine of an angle of 90° is 1. The sine of an angle of 180° degrees is zero, and the sine of an angle of 270° is -1. So the cycle starts at 0° and reaches its max at 90°, comes back to equilibrium at 180°, and on down to its minimum at 270° and back to equilibrium at its starting position to complete 360° of motion.

Now, the cosine of an angle of 0° is 1, which is the maximum value. Professor Weston uses cosine values in his method because he measures waves from peak to peak. That is, the start and end of the wave corresponds to 0° and 360° respectively. Measuring from peak to peak, 0° corresponds to the top of the circle, 90° to the far left, 180° at the bottom, 270° to the far right, and back to 360° at the top. Please refer to the image below. As you can see, the values between -1 and 1 remain in the same place. It is the cosine values that Weston uses to graph angular motion.

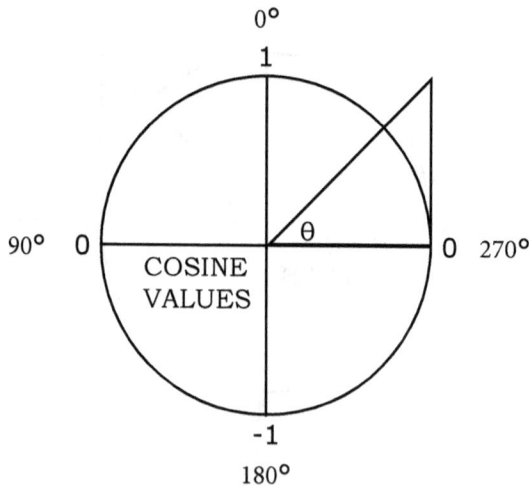

Professor Weston goes on to say that angular motion can be expressed algebraically by the simple equation:

$$y = \cos x$$

For every angle x, the cosine of that angle equals y. Or, he says that you can be a little more elaborate and put:

$$y = \cos(nt + e)$$

The variable "n" is the angle described by a moving point on the circle in the unit of time, which is "t". The variable "e" is the angle of epoch, which is the point from where you start measuring. In the above example, it is 0°. If for example, "n" is equal to 30°, and "t" is equal to "1", then y = cos (30°). When "t" is "2", y = cos (60°).

Using the circular image from the previous page, the linear chart below illustrates the relationship between orbital or cyclical motion and linear representation.

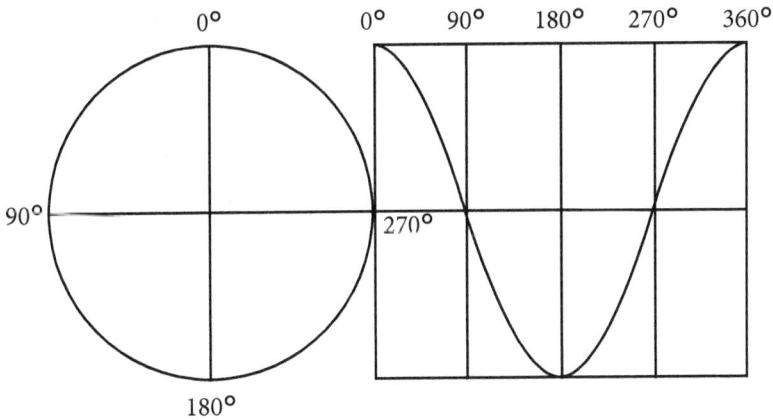

Continuing with where I left off, Professor Weston continues his example by constructing a cosine curve of 20.538 years along with the 7th harmonic of 20.538 years, which is 2.934 years. For more details, I refer to the reader to Professor Weston's book. What I would like the reader to take away from this is that you can construct a curve for any cyclical period desired and project that curve into the future.

In summary, Professor Weston's method of identifying the most dominant cycles within the data by his cut-and-try method indeed simplifies the method propounded by Henry Ludwell Moore. This leads me to the second set of questions mentioned earlier, what is the time factor, and what is the cause behind market movements?

Earlier, I quoted material where Gann stated that the cause of the 30-year cycle was the planet Saturn. We could interpret this to mean that time cycles are caused by planetary motion. In addition, we also have material where Gann has stated that he thought market movements to be cyclical. That said, can we also say that Gann thought that the cause behind market movements is planetary influence? It is this very idea that is supported by Professor Weston. On page 11 of *Forecasting the New York Stock Market* he writes,

> "It would probably become irksome to the reader if I labored through numerous pages of details in regard to the various studies and researches that I carried out during about 15 years of work on the problem, therefore, it comes best to briefly remark that all my research tended strongly to indicate that the stock market average price curve rises and falls in ACCORD WITH PLANETARY INFLUENCE. . . we now know what causes the principal long-swing movement in stocks. It is the varying distances between the two great planetary masses called JUPITER AND SATURN."

The planets Jupiter and Saturn produce a synodic cycle of approximately twenty years and this is the period that Weston is referring to.

The heliocentric orbital period of Saturn is on average approximately 29.4571 years while that of Jupiter is on average approximately 11.8618 years in length. If they started out in conjunction, it would take approximately twenty years for Jupiter to catch up to Saturn to form another conjunction. Mathematically, you can take the orbital periods of Jupiter and Saturn to calculate this period. Let "S" equal the orbital period of Saturn and "J" equal the orbital period of Jupiter. Then you have the following equation ensuring that you subtract the smaller orbital period from the larger.

$$\frac{S * J}{S - J} = \frac{29.4571 * 11.8618}{29.4571 - 11.8618} = \frac{349.4142}{17.5953} =$$

19.8584 or rounded to 19.86 years.

In Gann's *Method For Forecasting the Stock Market* Course dated January 17, 1932, he writes,

> *"The most important Time cycle is the 20-year cycle, or 240 months and most stocks and averages work closer to this cycle than any other. . . The next important major cycle is 30 years, which is caused by the planet Saturn. This planet makes one revolution around the sun every 30 years. Saturn rules the products of the earth and causes extreme high or low prices in products of the earth at the end of each 30-year cycle, and this makes Stocks high or low. The most important cycle of all is the 20-year cycle."*

Here we find that Gann identifies the 20-year cycle as the most important Time cycle and even reiterates this after talking about the Saturn Cycle of 30 years. So both Gann and Weston identified the 20 year cycle as the one that most stocks and averages work closer to than any other cycle. More importantly, we know that it is caused by planetary influence. In Rule 9 under his Rules for Forecasting in the same course, Gann writes,

> *"There is a major cycle of 30 years, which runs out three ten-year cycles. The 10-year cycle back from the present and the 20-year cycle have the most effect on the future."*

In Gann's *Master Time Factor and Forecasting by Mathematical Rules* course dated November 1935, he writes under the heading of Great Cycle - Master Time Period - 60 years:

> *"This is the greatest and most important cycle of all, which repeats every 60 years or at the end of the third 20-year cycle.*

After three synodic cycles of Jupiter and Saturn, they form a conjunction in the same relative portion of the zodiac. On average it takes three periods of 19.8584 years to complete this cycle, which is 59.5752 years. I believe that this is the 60-year cycle that Gann is referring to. Under the section heading of Master 20-Year Forecasting Chart 1831 - 1935, he writes,

> *"In order to make up an annual forecast, you must refer to my Master 20-year Forecasting Chart and see how the*

cycles have worked out and repeated in the past. And stated before, the 20-year cycle is the most important cycle for forecasting future market movements. It is one-third of the 60 year cycle and when three 20-year cycles run out, important bull and bear campaigns terminate."

From all that has been presented, this seems to answer the question, what is the cause behind market movements? Professor Weston and Gann both point to the importance of the 20-year cycle, which is caused by Jupiter and Saturn.

3

THE TIME FACTOR

The last of the questions has to do with the Time Factor. What is the Time Factor that Gann said Moore failed to get? What immediately stands out is that Gann talked about the Time Factor along with the cause behind market movements as if they were somehow related. Thus, the last piece of evidence connects the 20-year cycle to the Master Time Factor. In *My Story - The Search for W.D. Gann's Master Time Factor* an author going by the name, The Seeker, provides his evidence as to why the Master Time Factor is the 60-year cycle, which is 3 periods of 20 years. On page 33 he writes,

> *"I was reading an old copy of Mr. Gann's lesson entitled simply "FORECASTING". . . when I read the lesson on forecasting that he wrote in August 1939 and which is the same, word for word, that is in the stock course today; I noticed that it was different from the one that I was reading that he had written in 1935. But the thing that really caught my attention was where he was describing on page F-9 of the lesson how he had set up his "master forecasting chart". . . In my ephemeris I read CONJUNC-*

TIONS OF JUPITER AND SATURN - October 21, 1861, April 18, 1881, November 28, 1901, September 10, 1921, August 8 and October 20, 1940 and February 15, 1941 (triple conj.), February 19, 1961, January 1 and March 8 and July 24, 1981, and May 26, 2000. My friends, a cold shudder came over me as I realized with crystal clear and vivid awareness that I was READING THE elusive, legendary, much sought, "MASTER TIME FACTOR".

So the question becomes, how did The Seeker arrive at such a conclusion? What evidence is provided to support this claim? What The Seeker does is provide evidence from Gann's own writings to support his conclusion that the 60-year cycle is the Master Time Factor. I refer the reader to that book/pamphlet to see how the author lays out the argument to support this theory. However, I will say that the most important piece of evidence that he provides is in the comparison of an advertisement brochure for Gann's courses and the wording Gann used in the actual course itself.

In the brochure referenced, which is advertising the course, Gann says,

". . . and my secret discovery of the Master Time Factor and a new way of Forecasting by Mathematical Rules that are simple and practical."

In the actual course from November 1935, under the section on the 1926 Forecast, he says,

"According to my discovery of the 60 year-cycle . . .".

The Seeker connects this to the same way Gann described the Master Time Factor in the advertisement brochure as a "discovery". Thus, "Master Time Factor" and "60-year cycle" are both associated with the word "discovery" in the advertisement brochure and the actual course.

I have since attempted to do a search for the word "discovery" in Gann's other courses to see if he used that word in relationship to other things, and I could not find one instance of this word in his courses except in the instance being cited with respect to the 60-year cycle. I can't say that I have exhausted all possibilities to see if the word is used in other places outside of the courses, but I will say that one place it is used is in connection with his great mathematical discovery of 1908. In his promotional booklet entitled, *Why Money is Lost on Commodities and Stocks and How to Make Profits* from 1954, it records the following:

> *"1908 May 12th left Oklahoma City for New York City. August 8th made one of his greatest mathematical discoveries for predicting the trend of stocks and commodities. Started trading with a capital of $300 and made $25,000. Started another account with $130 and made $12,000 in thirty days time."*

There are many who think he is referring to his Master Time Factor. In the e-book entitled, *W.D. Gann on The Master Time Factor* published by the Gann Study Group, the author gives some background information on the Master Time Factor as follows:

> *"The first known reference to the Master Time Factor by*

that name appears to have been on July 9, 1927, in a letter by Mr. Gann, which has survived and been made public (not having access to everything that he wrote before that date we cannot be sure of when the first reference actually occurred).

In the letter to John H. Spohn, Gann wrote as follows:

"My latest discovery - the Master Time Factor - will be taught you."

In The Morning Telegraph of New York, New York, December 17, 1922, Gann says,

"My discovery of the time factor enables me to tell in advance when these extremes must, by the law of supply and demand, occur in stocks and commodities."

This is just a small sample of the word "discovery" and its connection to the Time Factor. If you are able to get the e-book, *W.D. Gann on The Master Time Factor*, you will find many more examples just like the quote from above. The word "discovery" seems to consistently be associated with the Master Time Factor, and one of the only places where he does not use it along with "Mathematical Discovery", "Master Time Factor" or "Time Factor", he uses it in connection with the 60-year cycle.

Seeing how this word was used in connection with the words listed above, I found it of interest to see how he used this word in his novel, *The Tunnel Thru the Air*. The first instance is on page 41 where it reads,

"Robert wrote to Walter telling him that he had been to Sherman to see Marie, that they had made up and that he was supremely happy. He confided to Walter his hopes of a great discovery and told him that with the love of Marie and her faith in him there was nothing he could not do."

So early in the story the main character is hoping for a great discovery. Then on page 94, we find the following,

"He wrote Marie how the market was working out according to his prediction; how the money was piling up; and that he would soon have money to start on his invention and new discovery."

At this point in the story it reads as if he has made his discovery, which was described as being new. On page 197, we find the following passage,

"On Sunday, June 19, 1927, Robert Gordon spent the day studying his charts and working out his cycles for stocks, cotton and grain. He was short of Major Motors and was watching it very closely. On this day he made a new and great discovery of a time factor from which he figured that Major Motors would decline until about June 30th and then start an advance which would last until about September 16th, 1927, when the Company would be 19 years old and at that time the stock would reach final high and would then go down to February to April, 1929."

Once again, we find that Gann connects "Time Factor" to the words "great discovery". The same words used on page 41 when he confided to Walter his hopes of a great discovery. On page 199, we find the following,

> *"His great discovery of what stocks would do at a certain age enabled him to make enormous profits when stocks reached the age where they would have fast moves up or down in a very short time."*

This time, "great discovery" is used in connection with what it enables him to do, similar to the description of what the Master Time Factor is described as enabling you to do. The next time we find the words "great discovery" is on page 238 in connection with the Pocket Radio. If you continue connecting the words "great discovery" and "great discoveries" in the novel, you will find that it is also connected with Walter's sleeping gas. I don't want to get to far off subject, but with the use of these words, I wonder if the description of the Pocket Radio and Sleeping Gas are veils to how the Master Time Factor works. Furthermore, could they somehow be related to the 60 year cycle?

In the e-book entitled, *W.D. Gann on The Master Time Factor*, published by the Gann Study Group, you can find numerous references describing what the Master Time Factor can do. For example, it can tell you when stocks will reach top or bottom, it can enable you to tell when time cycles run out, it can tell you when accumulation or distribution is taking place, and when to take profits and buy again. In addition, there are many references describing it as scientific and mathematical, but it is hard to find any reference as to what it is. Fortunately, I was able to find an advertisement that seems to do just that.

On page 32 of *Forbes* from 1952, there is an advertisement that reads,

"FORECAST MAJOR MARKET TOPS AND BOTTOMS -dates for TREND CHANGES with the MASTER TIME FACTOR! Only W. D. Gann Research, Inc., offers the Master Time Factor, a mathematical formula for predicting market tops and bottoms . . ."

age 32

with

The MASTER
TIME FACTOR!.

Only W. D. Gann Research, Inc. offers the Master Time Factor, a mathematical formula for predicting market tops and bottoms . . . perfected through more than 45 years of use

Although the screenshot is very grainy, the advertisement very clear states that it is a mathematical formula. This is very different from just saying it is a 60-year cycle. If indeed it is associated with the 60-year cycle, it seems to also involve a calculation.

I would also like to point out that the advertisement comes from W.D. Gann Research Inc. in 1952. I found the following from an article entitled, William Gann - A Legend,

"Sometime in 1947, Gann sold W. D. Gann Research, Inc. to C. C. Loosli, a San Francisco attorney. He became disenchanted with the business and on February 14, 1948, W. D. Gann Research, Inc. was transferred to Mr. Joseph L. Lederer of St. Louis, Missouri. The office for W. D. Gann Research, Inc. was maintained at 82 Wall Street in New York until 1952. Then it was moved to Scarsdale, New York, and in 1956 relocated to St. Louis, Missouri, where its only business was that of investment adviser."

Thus, at the time of the advertisement, I would assume that it was in the hands of Joseph Lederer who had acquired the business from C. C. Loosli. Is it possible that when C.C. Loosli acquired the business, he also acquired knowledge of the Master Time Factor, and when it was transferred to Joseph L. Lederer, did he also acquire knowledge of what the Master Time Factor was in order to describe it in the advertisement as a mathematical formula?

What I find interesting is that Gann's master calculators were also described using the words "mathematical formula". From September 29, 1953 there is a course entitled *W.D. Gann Mathematical Formula for Market Predictions*. It is described as The Master Mathematical Price Time and Trend Calculator. This was his plastic square of 144 overlay. I can't help but wonder if the information displayed in these calculators contain all the variables for the mathematical formula that Gann may have used as his Master Time Factor.

In fact, maybe there is something more to these calculators than meets the eye, and these calculators are what Gann describes as the Master Time Factor.

In Gann's promotional booklet entitled, *Why Money is Lost on Commodities and Stocks and How to Make Profits* from 1954, there is a section with the heading MATHEMATICAL PREDICTION FORMULA. There are four factors listed, which are TIME, PRICE, VOLUME, AND SPEED. Interestingly, Gann mentions various combinations of these factors as far back as 1933. It will be extremely beneficial to trace Gann's reference to these factors throughout the years with the aim of getting a better understanding of how he may have used them. Furthermore, evidence seems to point to the fact that these four factors are associated with what Gann describes as his mathematical prediction formula, and we have evidence that describes the Master Time Factor as a mathematical formula.

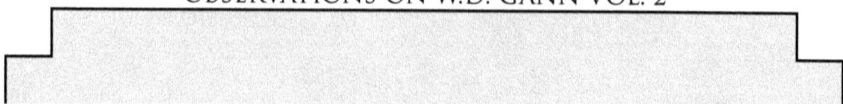

4

PRICE - TIME - VOLUME - VELOCITY

In the e-book entitled, *W.D. Gann on The Master Time Factor* published by the Gann Study Group, there is a reference to an advertisement in the Tampa Tribune of Tampa, Florida, dated January 22, 1933. On page 26 of the e-book it reads,

> *"Because you did not Know the Master Time Factor and relation of TIME to PRICE and VOLUME, which every investor and trader should KNOW. You have bought WHEN you should have sold short. . . By studying and learning when to BUY and SELL according to TIME, PRICE and VOLUME of Sales. Then you will trade on Mathematical Science and no longer guess and gamble on hope."*

On page 30 of the same e-book, there is another reference to these factors in the Times Picayune of New Orleans, Louisiana, dated June 8, 1933.

> *"You lose money trading because you do not know the rules the silent men of Wall Street use and the Master*

*Time Factor and relation of TIME to PRICE and VOLUME
of sales, which every investor and trader should KNOW"*

A little over five years later, we find on page 49 of the same e-book another reference to these factors in the Milwaukee Journal of Milwaukee, Wisconsin dated July 3, 1938. It reads,

"The movement of stock prices obeys a mathematical law of cycles which can be forecast by the Master Time Factor - Time is the most important element. When time is up, volume starts and velocity increases and prices move up or down."

The fourth reference to these factors is located in Gann's 1955 course entitled, *Master Calculator for Weekly Time Periods*. There is a section in the course with the heading, TIME, PRICE, VOLUME, VELOCITY, PITCH OR TREND. With respect to these factors it says,

"When a Time Cycle is completed, Volume increases and the market begins to move up faster or move down faster. The pitch or trend is determined by the 45° angle, which is most important, but other angles can be used to determine the trend. The pitch or trend is the 4th dimension and shows whether the market is slow or fast by the angles, whether very acute or above the 45° angle or flat and slow, below the 45° angle, which causes a slow creeping market and may later regain important angles and increase the pitch of the angle and start moving up faster."

In summary, these are the important points worth noting from the four sources above.

Every investor and trader should know the relation of Time to Price and Volume. Based on the words used in these sources, we have the following relationships:

1. TIME
"When Time is up" or "When a Time Cycle is Completed"

2. VOLUME
"Volume Starts" or "Volume Increases"

3. SPEED OR VELOCITY
"Velocity Increases" or "the market begins to move up faster or down faster"

4. PRICE
"Prices Move Up or Down"

First, I would like to start with what Gann refers to as SPEED or VELOCITY. In physics, the formula for speed is distance divided by time. For example, if the distance traveled is 60 miles, and the time elapsed is 1 hour, then 60 divided by 1 hour would give us a speed of 60 miles per hour. Velocity is equivalent to a specification of speed, but it should also include a direction. Thus, if I were to specify velocity I would have to say for example, 60 miles per hour traveling North.

In a distance versus time graph, distance is plotted on the y-axis and is usually measured in Miles or Meters, etc. TIME is plotted on the x-axis and can be measured in seconds, minutes, hours, etc. The graph below represents an object that is not moving. It is at rest. The straight horizontal line shows that its distance stays the same value as time progresses.

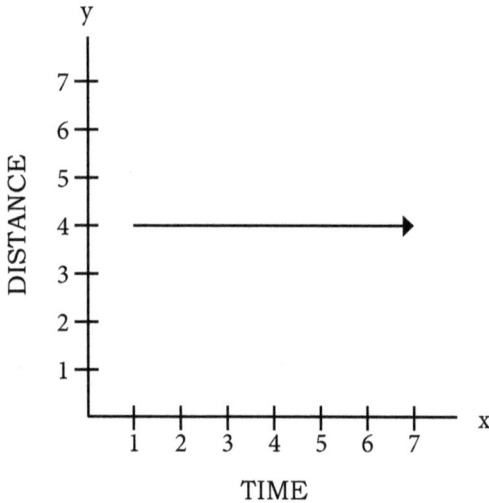

A straight line sloping upwards or downwards shows that the objects distance increases as time progresses. Please refer to the graph on the opposite page. Since it is moving it has velocity. Thus, the slope of these types of graphs gives you the VELOCITY. A straight upwards or downwards sloping line shows that the object has a constant velocity. Thus, the slope of the line shows how fast the object is moving. The greater the slope or angle, the greater the velocity.

   A stock chart is similar to a distance versus time graph. Time is measured in trading days, weeks, or months, and distance is measured in cents. When we draw a line connecting a low to a high price, we take the difference in

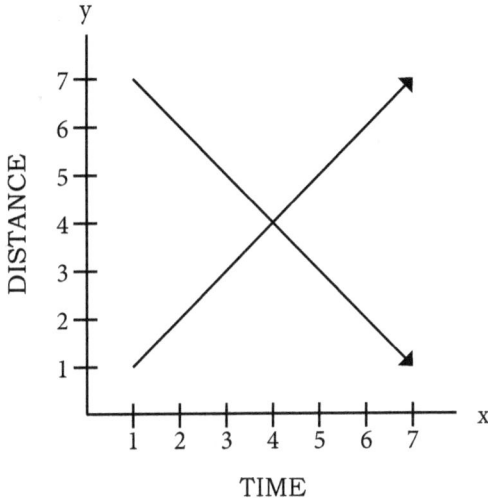

TIME

price, and divide it by the difference in time. Thus, the price change divided by the time change gives you the velocity of a move. Not to be forgotten is the fact that in order to specify velocity, you have to give a direction. On a stock chart the direction can be designated by the angle. Now, with respect to Gann material, I have read many instances where velocity has been confused with vibration as they are not the same thing.

For example, in an article entitled, *Rediscovering Gann's Law of Vibration* by James Smithson, he notes the start of the up trend for September Wheat is January 26, 1909. The article says that the contract expired on September 30, 1909. There are 247 days between these two dates. On January 26, 1909 the price was 94 cents, and on September 30, 1909 it sold as high as 120 cents. The difference in price is 26 cents. In the article, it says,

"Gann identified the long-term rate of vibration of this uptrend, which was .1053 cents per day (or 1 cent per 9.5 days)"

Although not detailed in the article, the .1053 cents per day is calculated by taking the difference in the price for those dates and dividing by the number of days elapsed. Thus, 26/247 = .105263, which is .1053 rounded to the fourth decimal place. The author describes this value as the long-term rate of vibration, but this is average speed, or velocity when given with the corresponding direction or angle.

With this understanding, if we go back to review what Gann says about velocity, it makes a lot more sense.

"When time is up, volume starts and velocity increases and prices move up or down."

"When a Time Cycle is completed, Volume increases and the market begins to move up faster or move down faster. The pitch or trend is determined by the 45° angle, which is most important, but other angles can be used to determine the trend. The pitch or trend is the 4th dimension and shows whether the market is slow or fast by the angles, whether very acute or above the 45° angle or flat and slow, below the 45° angle, which causes a slow creeping market and may later regain important angles and increase the pitch of the angle and start moving up faster."

When velocity or the slope increases, prices do indeed move up or down faster.

In mathematics, velocity is sometimes associated with wavelength, which is a term that Gann also used in one of his writings. On pages 39 - 41 of the 1929 Annual Stock Forecast supplement in *Wall Street Stock Selector* we find the following:

> *"I can teach you how to determine the wave lengths of different stocks so you will know about how many points they are going to advance when they go into new territory and about how many points they are going to decline when they break out of the zone of distribution. . . Each stock moves according to its individual time limit and makes top and bottom at different times, because the vibration and wave length varies on the different stocks."*

Waves may be graphed as a function of time or distance. From the distance graph, the wavelength may be determined.

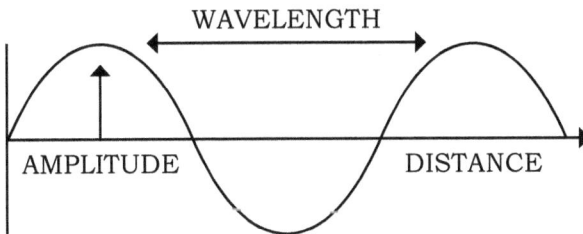

From the time graph, depicted on the following page, the period and frequency can be determined. From both together, the wave speed can be determined.

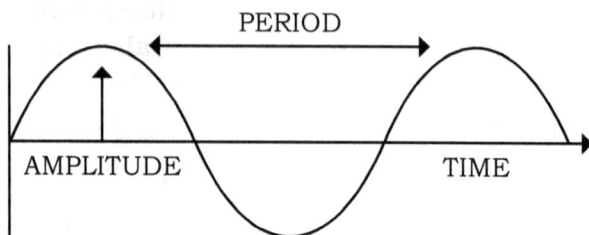

As stated before, a stock chart is a distance versus time graph. Time is measured on the x-axis as shown in the graph above. That being so, the period and frequency can be obtained by measuring time on the x-axis, and the wavelength can be obtained by measuring distance on the y-axis for this type of graph.

The period of a wave is the time to complete one vibrational cycle. So in the graph above, it would be the time from one peak to the next peak, which completes a cycle. From "Frequency and Period of a Wave",

> "Frequency and period are distinctly different, yet related, quantities. Frequency refers to how often something happens. Period refers to the time it takes something to happen. Frequency is a rate quantity. Period is a time quantity."

Therefore, frequency can be defined as something like cycles per second or vibrations per second. As such, the frequency is the reciprocal of the period and the period is the reciprocal of the frequency.

PERIOD = 1/FREQUENCY   FREQUENCY = 1/PERIOD

The rate of vibration is defined by the frequency. So what exactly is vibration? In an article entitled, *Frequency, Vibration and Oscillation - The Energy Patterns That Affect Your Wellbeing,* Pao L. Chang distinguishes vibration as follows:

> *"People sometimes use vibration and frequency interchangeably but they do have their differences. Vibration occurs when energy contracts toward the center point from which it first came out of. Oscillation happens when energy expands away from the center point. Frequency is achieved when one pattern or cycle of vibration and oscillation occurs. In other words, when an energy unit is done contracting and expanding, it has created one frequency pattern."*

Based on the information presented above, we see that vibration is related to frequency. So when Gann used the word vibration, I personally think he meant it in the mathematical sense as being related to frequency. To summarize, on the distance versus time graph the period and frequency can be obtained by measuring time on the x-axis. Now, the wavelength can be obtained by measuring distance on the y-axis. In fact, distance and wavelength are the same thing.

Earlier, I stated that in mathematics, velocity is sometimes associated with wavelength. Speed or velocity can also be defined as wavelength divided by the period, which is exactly the same as distance divided by the time. In addition, since frequency is the reciprocal of the period, velocity can also be defined as distance/wavelength multiplied by the frequency/rate of vibration.

When Gann said that he could teach you how to determine the wave lengths of different stocks, he said it with the caveat that you will know about how many points they are going to advance when they go into new territory and about how many points they are going to decline when they break out of the zone of distribution. This is exactly what distance is on a stock chart. It is the change in price on the y-axis.

As an example, I have shown a low to a high for stock symbol NWBO. The low was on 12/19/2013 at 320 cents. The high was on 3/11/2014 at 1064 cents. The distance or wavelength is 744 cents and the time or period is 54 trading days. Thus, The average speed is 13.78 cents per trading day. Or if specifying average velocity using the values above, it would be 13.78 cents per trading day at 85.848 degrees. If speed is also equal to the distance or wavelength times the frequency, then 744 multiplied by .0185185 (1/54) gives us the same value of 13.78. You can readily prove that if the velocity increases, the price would move up faster. Take 15 cents per trading day and multiply by 54 and you get 810, which is indeed greater than 744. The relationship between VELOCITY and PRICE is therefore proven.

Moving on, the next component that we need to analyze is VOLUME. Gann said that when volume starts or volume increases, velocity increases or prices move up or down faster. The relationship between VOLUME and VELOCITY is somewhat obvious. Volume records the amount of buying and selling activity recorded for a particular stock. The greater this activity, the greater the velocity whether on the up or down side.

On page 9 of the e-book entitled, *W.D. Gann on The Master Time Factor*, there is a passage from Gann that reads as follows:

> *"The VOLUME OF SALES is the real driving power behind the market and shows whether Supply or Demand is increasing or decreasing."*

Gann indicated that it was through the study of volume that revealed the balance between supply and demand. Throughout the e-book referenced above, you will find many references to SUPPLY AND DEMAND from Gann's advertisements. In the same e-book there is reference to an advertisement in *The Plain Dealer* of Cleveland, Ohio from May 15, 1921. It reads,

> *"SUPPLY AND DEMAND always govern prices in the end. When Supply exceeds Demand, stocks decline; when Demand exceeds Supply, they advance."*

So what is the mathematical relationship between VOLUME OF SALES and VELOCITY? In other words, what causes a change in velocity from a mathematical perspective.

First and foremost, it is important to understand that in physics, the rate at which an object changes its velocity is called acceleration. In other words, an object is accelerating if it is changing its velocity. If an object is changing its velocity by the same amount each unit of time, it is referred to as constant acceleration. To calculate acceleration, you take the change in velocity and divide by the time elapsed.

$$\text{Avg. Acceleration} = \frac{\Delta \text{ velocity}}{\text{time}} = \frac{v_f - v_i}{t}$$

Please note, the change in velocity is the final velocity minus the initial velocity. Possessing the definition for a change in velocity, the next question to answer is what causes an object to accelerate.

This led me to Newtonian Mechanics and the 2nd of Newton's three laws of motion. From "Newton's Second Law" from www.physicsclassroom.com, I found the following:

> *"According to Newton, an object will only accelerate if there is a net or unbalanced force acting upon it. The presence of an unbalanced force will accelerate an object - changing its speed, its direction, or both its speed and direction."*

This seemed to fit in perfectly with the concept of supply and demand if viewed as forces. When demand is greater than supply, the difference in how much demand is greater than supply could very well correspond to the net or unbalanced force described by Newton. A net force of this type would cause an acceleration where prices would increase. On the other hand, when supply is greater than demand there is also an unbalanced force, but this type will cause prices to decrease. We can also see that when supply and demand are in equilibrium, prices remain the same. It is only when they are unbalanced, where one force is greater than the other that causes a change in velocity and price.

Consider Gann's words in the supplementary publicity material to *Wall Street Stock Selector*, p. 44.

> *"I study the market daily to determine a change in SUP-PLY and DEMAND and to locate the balance of power, in order that my subscribers may get the benefit of big moves."*

In light of what has just been presented, this comment makes a whole lot of sense. If one could somehow determine from Volume of Sales how much one force was greater than the other, I imagine that you could predict how big of a corresponding move was expected to come.

With an understanding of the relationships above, I looked for the math that would explain how much an object would accelerate based on the force applied. On the site www.physicsclassroom.com, it went on to say,

> *"The acceleration of an object depends directly upon the net force acting upon the object, and inversely upon the mass of the object."*

This means that when the force acting on an object is increased, the acceleration of the object is also increased, but as the mass of an object is increased, the acceleration of the object is decreased. Taking both into consideration, the equation for acceleration is equal to the net force divided by the mass of an object.

$$a = F_{net}/m$$

This is rearranged from the more familiar equation, force equals mass times acceleration.

$$F_{net} = m * a$$

In all honesty, this posed a big stumbling block for me. My initial thought was that stocks don't have mass, yet it is an integral part of Newton's equation. At this point in my research, the best thing I could do was to attempt to understand how Gann may have used volume to locate what he called - the balance of power. Maybe this would help me to better understand the mathematical relationship between volume and velocity. For this purpose, two of the best resources come from Gann's book entitled, *Truth of the Stock Tape*, and the other from a course entitled, *Method For Forecasting the Stock Market,* dated January 17, 1931.

In *Method For Forecasting the Stock Market*, there is a section with the heading, Vanadium Steel, Weekly High & Low Chart, Volume of Sales. Gann provides a description of a chart where you not only have the usual price and time components, but also volume. I have never seen a chart that tracks all three components like Gann describes it in this course. The chart begins September 29, 1928 and for each space $^1/_8$ inch wide represents 25,000 shares.

Time is plotted in the normal fashion where every $1/8$ inch is equal to 1 week. Now, consider what Gann says regarding the following.

> *"From the low on November 13, to the high in April, the total volume of sales was 1,672,600 shares figuring 25,000 to each $1/8$ space to move over each week would bring this over to the 67th space . . ."*

To calculate this he took the total volume of sales from November 13 to the high in April and divided by 25,000. Thus, 1,672,600 divided by 25,000 is equal to 66.904. Rounded up it is equal to the 67th space on the chart. Then he gives us the following:

> *"In the weeks of May 3rd and 10th, the total volume was 614,000 shares, bringing the grand total up to that time to 2,282,000 which brings it to space 91, on the week ending May 10th and puts our volume chart 6 spaces too far over."*

If you add 614,000 shares to 1,672,600, you actually get 2,286,600 instead of 2,282,000. Regardless, both figures will put you a little over 91 spaces. 2,286,600 divided by 25,000 is equal to 91.464 and 2,282,000 divided by 25,000 is equal to 91.28. What is interesting is that he says it is 6 spaces too far over.

The chart begins September 29, 1928 and he references the week ending May 10, 1930. September 29, 1928 was a Saturday, and based on the numbers given, I have to assume that September 29, 1928 is the end of the first week.

Therefore, the beginning of that first week would start on September 22, 1928. So from September 22, 1928 to May 10, 1930 there are 595 days. If you Divide 595 by the 7 days in a week, you get 85 weeks, which is 6 less than 91. So with respect to time, it is May 10, 1930, which is a total of 85 weeks from the beginning, but with respect to volume, it is ahead of time by 6 weeks at 91 weeks over from the beginning.

So the way the chart works, it appears that volume can be ahead of or behind time, and he analyzes volume with respect to the angles based on its own position on the chart. To further validate this, we also have the following passage:

> *"Bringing the total number of sales up to the week ending June 7, we have 3,170,800 shares. This would bring us to the space 126, marked in red ink, and the way we have the volume chart, it is 8 spaces too far over."*

3,170,800 divided by 25,000 is equal to 126.832, which Gann apparently rounds down to 126. This seems to make sense, but what follows does not. September 22, 1928 to June 7, 1930 is 623 days. 623 days divided by the 7 days in a week is only 89 weeks. 126 minus 89 is 37 spaces too far over. Maybe there is a typo or something was transcribed incorrectly. Of the many things I tried, the one that seems to make more sense is that space 126 should have read 127. This is supported by the math because 126.832 is closer to 127 than 126 when rounded. Furthermore, when you subtract 89 weeks from 127, you get 38. So instead of 8 spaces too far over, maybe it should have said 38 spaces too far over. Despite the discrepancies, the point being made is that volume can be in a different position than time.

Later on in the course under the section entitled, Fast Advances and Fast Declines, he explains what happens when volume breaks an angle before space.

"For example, make up a volume chart on U.S. Steel weekly from May 31, 1929 to date, and you will see that it broke so sharply after the high in September, 1929, because the volume broke the angle before the angles were broken by the weekly or monthly chart."

It would be a good exercise to plot volume in a similar fashion to Vanadium Steel to see what can be learned from a study of volume in this manner. That is, to see how price reacts when volume and price break angles at the same time, and when they break angles at different times with volume being ahead of or behind price.

Now that we understand how volume was plotted on the x-axis, we need to investigate how it was plotted on the y-axis. I personally did not see an obvious description of how it was plotted on the vertical y-axis in the course. However, if you go to http://www.wdgann.com/vault, and scroll through the images by clicking on the arrows on the right or left of the displayed image, you will come to one that reads, A Study in Volume - 1920. Based on what little can be seen in this image, I believe that the high and low price of the stock for the corresponding week is plotted on the y-axis. In my honest opinion, it looks very similar to what is called an EquiVolume box.

On the site http://stockcharts.com/school/doku. php?id=chart_school:chart_analysis:equivolume, I found the following information on "EquiVolume":

"Developed by Richard W. Arms Jr., EquiVolume is a price plot that incorporates volume into each period. . . An EquiVolume box consists of three components: price high, price low and volume. The price high forms the upper boundary, the price low forms the lower boundary and volume dictates the width."

The image below depicts the components of an EquiVolume box, which looks very similar to the boxes in the "A Study in Volume - 1920" image from http://www.wdgann.com/vault.

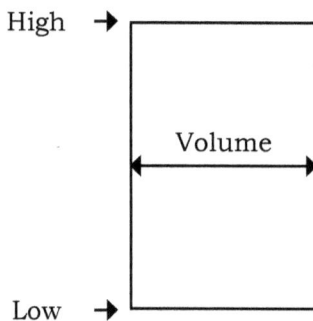

The difference between an Equivolume box and Gann's description of how he plotted volume has to do with the time axis. Gann's recording of volume was not limited to the time component. If there was a large amount of volume it could span more than one unit of time. Based on what I can tell, the time unit expands to accommodate the amount of volume being recorded with respect to the EquiVolume box.

Now that we understand how Gann may have plotted volume, there are several more examples that provide us with additional information on how he utilized volume in his analysis. In his analysis of Vanadium Steel with respect to an advance, Gann states,

". . . during the week of February 8, there was a small re-action, but the volume of sales was only 23,000 shares. The advance was resumed the following week and sales reached 62,400 shares. The next week the sales were 48,300 shares. Then during the week ending March 1, there was a small reaction but the volume of sales were only 36,500 shares which indicated that the buying was better than the selling, and that there was no heavy sell-ing pressure yet."

After this he says that the advance resumed. In this example, it appears that Gann compared the volume on the reaction, 36,500 shares, with the preceding week where sales were 48,300 shares, and came to the conclusion that demand was greater than supply.

In another example, we find a scenario that indicates when top is reached.

"During the week ending April 19th, sales were 184,600 shares and during the week ending April 26th, sales were 258,100 shares. With the stock up 105 points from the extreme low, and the volume of sales almost equal-ing the total amount of stock outstanding, was a plain indication that top was being reached for a big reaction."

After this, Gann says a big decline followed. In this example, we learn that Gann tracked the accumulated volume of sales with respect to the total amount of stock outstanding.

In the next example I would like to draw your attention to, we find the following:

> "... the stock declined to 87 during the week ending May 10th on sales of 310,400 shares, breaking all records up to that time. . . During the week ending May 10th, the volume of sales of 242,400 shares and the price crossed the top of the following week and advanced to 118 $^1/_4$. The following week it advanced to 120 $^1/_4$ on sales of 248,600 shares, showing that the volume of trading was increasing on the way up but the price was not increasing in proportion. During the week ending May 31st, the stock reached 124 on volume of sales of 135,700 shares, an indication that the selling was better than the buying and that when the price level approached where distribution started, it showed that there was again the very best of selling."

In this example there are two things worth noting. First, it appears that Gann compares the volume on the decline to the volume on the advance in the subsequent weeks. It first declined to 87 on sales of 310,400 shares. The following week it advanced on sales of 248,600 shares. During the week ending May 31, it advanced to 124 on volume of sales of 135,700 shares. Is it possible that Gann compared the decline on sales of 310,400 to the advance on sales of 248,600 and the next advance on sales of 135,700 and see that the selling was greater than the buying? The 310,400 shares on the decline are greater than 248,600 and also 135,700.

The second thing worth noting is that Gann appears to track volume of sales with respect to the corresponding price change. During the week of May 10 he says that the stock declined to 87. Then the following week after May 10 it climbed to 118 $^1/_4$ on shares of 242,400. 118 $^1/_4$ minus 87 is 31 $^1/_4$ points. If you divide 242,400 shares by 31 $^1/_4$ points, it would take 7756.8 points of volume to move the stock 1 point in price. The week after it reached 118 $^1/_4$, it climbed to 120 $^1/_4$ on 248,600 shares. 120 $^1/_4$ minus 118 $^1/_4$ is 2 points. Yet, the volume of sales was about the same as before at 248,600 shares. Dividing 248,600 by 2, you get 124,300. Therefore, it takes 124,300 points of volume just to move the stock 1 point in price. Hence the statement that volume of trading was increasing on the way up, but the price was not increasing in proportion. This is a sign that supply is greater than demand. There is plenty of stock for sale at this price level and investors could get all they wanted without bidding prices up.

In the section of the course under Fast Advances and Fast Declines there are more examples provided to describe what happens when Volume breaks angles ahead of or behind price.

"Why do stocks that have fast advances, reverse quickly and have sharp, quick declines before breaking the angle of 67 1/2°, or the 45° angle on the monthly and weekly charts? It is because the large volume of sales moves the prices over until the 45° angle is really broken at a very high level, which can be seen by making the combination time, space and volume chart. The volume chart shows that the angle is broken while the time chart, which only shows one space for each month or week, does not show the angle broken."

This was the paragraph given before Gann said that U.S. Steel weekly from May 31, 1929 broke so sharply after the high in September 1929 because volume broke the angle before the angles were broken by the weekly or monthly chart. By this, I think that he means that volume broke the angle before "price" broke the same angle, and this is why it broke so sharply.

There are a couple more examples in the course involving volume, but I will leave the rest for the reader to explore. For now I would like to leave the reader with this.

"When a stock is in a very weak, or a very strong position, it will always show it by its position on angles, and a volume chart, made up according to the proper spacing with volume, that is, considering the total number of shares, will show when the stock is in a strong or weak position and show whether buying or selling predominates, enabling you to determine whether supply is increasing, or whether demand is decreasing."

This strongly indicates that you can't judge whether a stock is in a strong or weak position with just price and time alone. Yet, when have you ever seen volume tracked the way Gann describes it in this course. Earlier, I provided examples from Gann's advertisements that showed just how important the study of volume was to Gann's work. One of these came from page 9 of the e-book entitled, *W.D. Gann on The Master Time Factor.*

"The VOLUME OF SALES is the real driving power behind the market and shows whether Supply or Demand is in-

creasing or decreasing."

I have to reinforce to the reader that it was through the study of volume that revealed the balance between supply and demand. As I mentioned on page 58, another great resource on how Gann utilized volume comes from his book entitled, *Truth of the Stock Tape.*

On page 6 of *Truth of the Stock Tape*, we find the following comments on volume to reinforce and add to what we have learned thus far.

"Market movements depend upon Supply and Demand. It requires volume of trading in proportionate large or small amounts to move stocks up or down. The volume of sales to the stock market is the same as the steam is to the locomotive or the gasoline is to the automobile. The sales are the motive power which drives prices up or down. For example: United States Steel has five million shares of common stock, and it requires a very large volume of sales to move this stock up or down very much. General Motors has fifty million shares of common stock and its fluctuations are confined to a very narrow range, because the buying or selling of 100,000 shares will not move it more than a point, if that much, while the buying of 100,00 shares of Baldwin will often move it up or down five or ten points, because there are only 200,000 shares of Baldwin outstanding and seldom ever over 100,000 shares of stock floating in the street. Therefore, in order to understand the meaning of volume, you must know the total capital stock outstanding and the floating supply of the stock you are trading in."

Gann then goes on to provide an example saying that when the floating supply of a stock is small with respect to the total capital stock outstanding, it will make larger moves compared to a stock that has a large floating supply with respect to its total capital stock outstanding. So what does Gann mean by floating supply?

Float or Floating Supply is defined as the number of shares available for trading a particular stock. It is calculated by subtracting closely-held shares, and restricted stock from a firm's total outstanding shares. So at any given time, there is only a certain amount available for trading. Equipped with an understanding of floating supply with respect to the total shares outstanding, we can move on to analyze some of the example situations Gann provides in his book.

On page 53 Gann provides us with a situation regarding U.S. Steel, but first let me provide you some of the details concerning this stock in order to put things in perspective. On page 6 and also on page 52 he tells us that U.S. Steel has 5 million shares of common stock, and on page 52 he tells us that at least one million or more shares must change hands before any big move will take place from any resistance level. This is obviously based on the floating supply, for which I tried to find a value for U.S. Steel in Gann's book, but did not see anything. In my opinion, if we knew the actual floating supply, I think it would make things more clear as to why he said one million or more shares must change hands before any big move would take place.

Moving on to the example, on page 53 of *Truth of the Stock Tape*, Gann says,

"Suppose U.S. Steel has advanced 20 or 30 points, and

it reaches a level where there are 200,000 shares in one day, but the stock only gains one point. The next day there are 200,000 shares and it makes no gain. This is plain enough that at this point the supply of the stock exceeds the demand, or at least that buyers are able to get all the stock they want without bidding prices up."

This is the same scenario mentioned on pages 63 to 64 of this book with respect to the example Gann provided in his course from 1931. Gann is tracking volume with respect to the price change and when there is large volume, but little price change, it is a sign that supply is greater than demand. There are more examples like the one presented above worth investigating, but I will leave that for the reader as I would now like to revisit the mathematical relationship between Volume and Velocity.

On page 58, I noted that the equation for acceleration, which is a change in the rate of velocity, is equal to the net force divided by the mass of an object.

$$a = F_{net}/m$$

I also stated that this posed a big stumbling block for me because my initial thoughts was that stocks don't have mass, yet it was an integral part of Newton's equation. I had searched for an equation or explanation for an acceleration that did not contain mass with no luck. Although I have been working on this book since February 2015, it was only upon waking on March 1, 2016 and thinking about the material on Volume from page 67 of this chapter that a possible solution seemed to present itself.

To explain what came to me, it would be best if I first provided a description on the properties of Mass. First and foremost, Mass and Weight are not the same thing. From http://www.physicsclassroom.com/class/newtlaws/Lesson-2/Types-of-Forces on "Types of Forces"

> "Many students of physics confuse weight with mass. The mass of an object refers to the amount of matter that is contained by the object; the weight of an object is the force of gravity acting upon the object. Mass is related to how much stuff is there and weight is related to the pull of the Earth (or any other planet) upon that stuff."

There is no doubt I was confusing Mass with Weight. It now makes sense that stocks don't have Weight as they are not affected by the force of gravity. However, Mass, which is related to how much stuff is there is a different story.

In Physics, we know that an unbalanced force causes an acceleration, which depends directly upon the net force, and also on inversely upon the object's mass. Using the equation on the previous page to determine the acceleration, lets say that we are applying a force of 100 Newtons to an object that has a mass of 10 kg. The acceleration is 10 m/s^2. Now, if we apply the same force to an object that has a mass of 50 kg, the acceleration is less at 2 m/s^2. This tells us that if the same force is applied, the object with more mass will not accelerate or change velocity as much as the object with less mass. Doesn't this sound like Gann's description of Total Outstanding Shares and FLOAT given on page 67? Revisiting page 6 of *Truth of the Stock Tape*, we find the following comments.

"For example: United States Steel has five million shares of common stock, and it requires a very large volume of sales to move this stock up or down very much. General Motors has fifty million shares of common stock and its fluctuations are confined to a very narrow range, because the buying or selling of 100,000 shares will not move it more than a point, if that much, while the buying of 100,00 shares of Baldwin will often move it up or down five or ten points, because there are only 200,000 shares of Baldwin outstanding and seldom ever over 100,000 shares of stock floating in the street. Therefore, in order to understand the meaning of volume, you must know the total capital stock outstanding and the floating supply of the stock you are trading in."

In this passage, Gann says that General Motors has fifty million shares of common stock and that it takes a very large volume of sales to move it up or down very much. As a result its fluctuations are confined to a very narrow range. Gann also says that the same force being applied, 100,000 shares in his example, will not move it more than a point, while the same force applied to Baldwin will often move it up or down five or ten points because there are only 200,000 shares outstanding and seldom ever over 100,000 shares of stock floating in the street. To me, this sounds very analogous to the example where we applied a force to an object with a mass of 50 kg, and the same force to one with a mass of 10 kg. The object with more mass doesn't change its rate of velocity as much as the object with less mass. What I am suggesting is that either the total outstanding shares of a stock or its FLOAT is equivalent to the mass of an object in Physics.

An unbalanced force acting upon an object with a specified mass is essentially the same as VOLUME acting on a stock with a certain amount of FLOAT. If we allow ourselves to accept that the number of outstanding shares for a particular stock is equivalent to the concept of Mass in physics, it will open the door for us to possibly grasp some of the other things Gann talked about. Consider for example the *Ticker and Investment Digest* article from 1909. In the article we find the following passage:

> *"The power to determine the trend of the market is due to my knowledge of the characteristics of each individual stock and a certain grouping of different stocks under their proper rates of vibration. Stocks are like electrons, atoms and molecules, which hold persistently to their own individuality in response to the fundamental law of vibration. Science has laid down the principle that the properties of an element are a periodic function of its atomic weight."*

In 1909, prior to the *Ticker and Investment Digest* article, there were a series of advertisements posted in the *New York Herald* that made statements similar to those of W.D. Gann. The advertisements only provided a business name with the title "OROLO", along with a street address. Although there is no authorship attached to the advertisements, we know that they were made by Gann based on their content. In the e-book entitled, *Who was OROLO?*, one advertisement dated Sunday, April 18, 1908 says,

> *"I find the different stocks grouped into families, each*

*having its own distinct vibration, which acts sympatheti-
cally upon others of the group and causes them to move
in unison."*

If I may summarize, we find Gann describing in both quoted
passages, a method by which he groups stocks into what he
describes as "families", which is based on their proper rates
of vibration. The analogy that Gann is drawing from with
respect to the word "families", comes from the elements of
chemistry, where elements in the same family show striking
resemblances among one another. In a book entitled, *On the
Discovery of the Periodic Law*, John Newlands states,

> *"In an appendix to the paper (Chemical News, vol. x. p.
> 94), August 20, 1864, I announced the existence of a sim-
> ple relation or law among the elements when arranged in
> the natural order of their atomic weights, to the effect that
> the eight element, starting from a given one, was sort of
> a repetition of the first, or that elements belonging to the
> same group stood to each other in relation similar to that
> between extremes of one or more octaves in music."*

Note that the elements were arranged by Newlands in the
natural order of their atomic weights. Atomic weight is an
older term that is equivalent to relative atomic mass. It is the
ratio of the average atomic mass of the different isotopes of
that element to the unified atomic mass unit. Mass Number
is slightly different as it is the number of neutrons plus pro-
tons. I don't want to get into the controversy of how each one
is supposed to be defined, but suffice to say that arranging
by mass displays a periodicity among the elements.

Could it be that Gann's reference to grouping stocks into certain families is based on their Total Outstanding Shares or either their FLOAT? In the *Ticker and Investment Digest* article it reads:

> *"Through the law of vibration every stock in the market moves in its own distinctive sphere of activities, as to intensity, volume and direction; all the essential qualities of its evolution are characterized in its own rate of vibration. Stocks, like atoms, are really centres of energy; therefore, they are controlled mathematically."*

This supports why Gann said you have to study individual stocks, and not averages. Stocks are unique and distinct. You have to understand how they move individually, and then you can connect them to the whole. Their individual movements are very much tied to their Total Outstanding Shares and floating supply as detailed by Gann from the quote on page 67. Can it also be said that the properties of a stock are a periodic function of its outstanding shares and floating supply?

Taking all of the above into consideration, one of the key questions that needs to be answered is how to properly scale a chart taking outstanding shares and floating supply into consideration. We saw earlier where Gann said that every 1/8th inch represented 25,000 shares for Vanadium Steel, but we don't know why he chose that number. I think it is tied to the outstanding shares and floating supply for Vanadium Steel during that time. I can honestly say, without a properly scaled chart, the Master Calculator will not provide you with what the course says it will.

Unfortunately, I don't know and easy way to determine the proper scale for a chart taking outstanding and floating shares into consideration. I will have to continue experimenting and testing different things in order to find a solution. Getting back to the main focus of this book, which is to understand the relationship between the four factors mentioned by Gann, I have provided a possible explanation for the mathematical relationship between Volume and Velocity. We will now take a look at the relationship between Time and Volume. Going back to our summary of the articles where Gann made reference to the four factors, he said that "When Time is up" or "When a Time Cycle is Completed", "Volume Starts" or "Volume Increases". What did Gann mean when he said, "When Time is up"? The most obvious reference that I found also came from his *Method For Forecasting the Stock Market* course dated January 17, 1931.

"As a general rule, when a change in trend takes place of importance, the volume of sales will show it. The volume of sales usually increases when a stock starts to advance from low levels, or from dullness, and the same after a long period of dullness at a high level, when activity starts on the down side, the volume of sales increases. . . With the daily, weekly and monthly high and low chart, the important angles cannot be crossed at extreme low levels, until proper time has elapsed, neither can important angles be broken at high levels until sufficient time has elapsed. Therefore, the angles are very important because when broken they usually mean that the time has run out, whether you know it or not, and a change in trend will take place."

In Gann's own words, when an angle is broken it usually means that time has ran out.

As Gann researchers, I know that at some point in your studies you have dealt with scaled charts. For example, if you are looking at a daily chart, then every unit of time is equal to say 1 cent in price. So a 45° angle would move at the rate of 1 cent every trading day. I'm sure I am not alone in wondering how applying a generic scale to a stock chart will accurately tell me that when an angle is broken, volume will increase. Using stock symbol NWBO as an example, if I use a scale of 1 cent per trading day, and I start the angle at the low on December 19, 2013, the 45° seems to rise too slow for the data being analyzed. It would take approximately nine to 10 months before this angle is broken and there is no clear indication of a change in trend or an increase in volume at the time the angle is broken.

I do understand that you could place additional angles on the chart that rise at a faster rate and are harmonics of the 1 X 1, but doing so shows that they don't in any way fit with how Gann described using them.

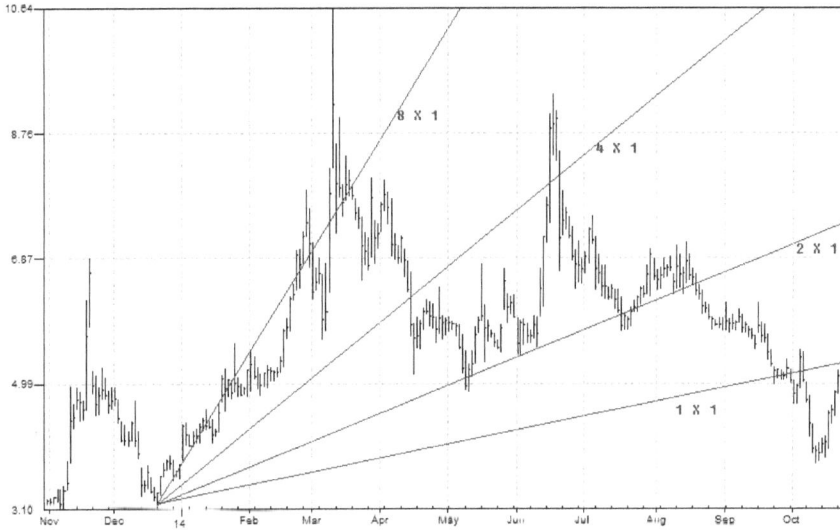

For example, looking at the 8 X 1 angle, the stock straddles it so that you can't tell whether it is breaking it or staying above the angle. Gann said that a change in trend and an increase in volume should accompany the breaking of an angle. This points to the fact that you just can't scale a chart using a generic scale. It has to fit the data, and it has to fit the data the way Gann described that it should.

Gann said that when a stock is trending up, it will make higher tops and higher bottoms. We know that the angle represents the velocity or speed of the movement. If we put on an angle from bottom, the low of the stock for each subsequent day should be able to stay above the angle if it is moving at that speed. This is quite different from drawing an angle from a low to a high price. Using the same example, if I draw an angle from the low price on December 19, 2013 and draw it so that it supports subsequent low prices, we get the following angle.

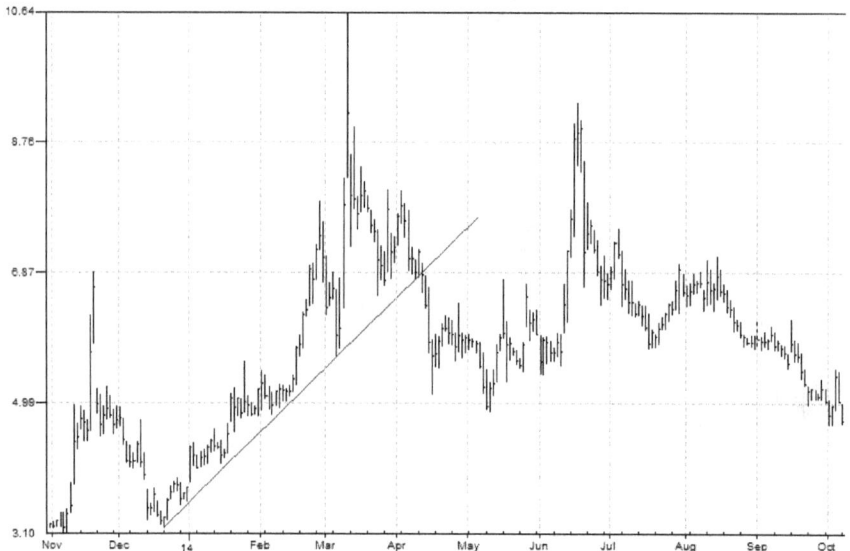

When we draw an angle like this, we can see that the stock does maintain the angle for some time, and when it finally does break the angle, the trend is changing. In addition, there is a corresponding increase in volume. April 10 is the line that you see that straddles the angle reaching above and below it. On that day volume was 1,057,500. On the three days before, volume was 488,000 on April 7, 571,000 on April 8, and 353,900 on April 9. The volume after April 10 was approximately two and a quarter times more than the average of the three days prior.

In the subsequent days after April 10, volume was 749,900 shares on April 11, and 1,348,800 on April 14, which definitely shows an increase in volume when the angle was broken. This is exactly what Gann said you would see when an important angle was broken. In this manner we are working backwards to figure out how to draw the angles so that they give us the information that Gann said they should. The next step is to calculate the speed or velocity of this angle.

To do so, I subtracted the low price on December 19, 2013 from the low where the angle crossed on March 6, 2014. So 565 - 320 gave me 245 cents. The number of trading days between these two dates is 51. Therefore, the average speed is 245 divided by 51, which is approximately 4.8 cents per trading day. This was close enough to 5 cents per trading day for me to round up, so I used this speed for my 1 X 1 angle. This means that 1 unit of price is equivalent to 5 cents. So the angle moves up at the rate of 1 unit of price, which is 5 cents, to 1 trading day. If you put on this angle and one of its harmonics you get the image on the following page.

The first thing that stands out is the fact that the stock revisits this angle and clips the top on June 17, 2014. There are some interesting relationships worth pointing out, but I am not implying anything by them. The time from the low on December 19, 2013 to April 9, 2014, which is the day before the stock closed significantly lower than the angle, is 75 trading days. When the stock revisited the angle on June 17, 2014, the time elapsed from December 19, 2013 was 122 trading days. 122 divided by Phi or 1.618 is 75.4. These two points share a mathematical relationship with respect to the corresponding angle.

In addition to the above, the stock bounces off the 1 X 16 angle on the October 10, 2014 low. If you take the 122 trading days and divide it by a perfect fifth, which is the musical ratio of 1.5, you get 81.333 trading days, which is the time from the June 17, 2014 high to the low in October. Getting back to the main subject, if you draw angles from more lows, you can definitely see how it corresponds to what Gann was talking about.

In the chart on the following page, there is a 4 X 1 angle from the low on November 7, 2013. Notice that at this speed, the stock maintains this angle as each subsequent low is able to stay above the angle, but when it does break the angle, there is a corresponding change in trend as the stock starts to work lower. Consider also that on November 18, 2013, which is the day before the top, the volume of sales was 5,602,500. The next day it was 4,267,600. The corresponding price change was 176 and 104 cents. Then on November 20, 2013, volume was 6,579,000, which is much more than he previous two days, but the corresponding price change was only 35 cents. As we have learned, this was a clear indication that the selling was greater than the buying and the trend turned down.

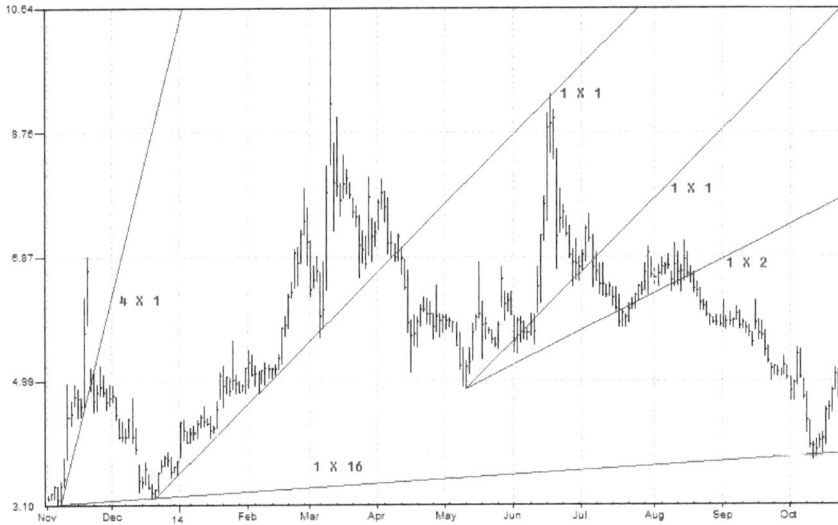

We can also see that when the stock broke the 1 X 2 angle from the low on May 9, 2014 the trend clearly changed. Referring to the chart on the next page, if we move to the right, we will also see that the stock revisits this same 1 X 2 angle on 7/23/2015. More importantly, the 1 X 2 angle from the October low shows how consistently the stock maintains this angle until it is broken on 8/19/2015 on heavy volume. You can even draw angles form the minor lows and get a clear indication that when these angle are broken, the trend changes. Consider the 2 X 1 from the low on 6/30/2015.

It is very clear that each subsequent low in July does not break this angle, but when it does, it does so on heavy volume and thereafter the trend changes.

We can use the same angles and draw them from tops, but in following our methodology there is a difference from when we draw them from lows. When a stock reaches top it usually does so on heavy volume sending the stock up a little further than normal. Keeping in mind that in order for the trend to be down, the stock must make lower tops and lower bottoms, but it is logical that if drawing angles from tops, that each subsequent top is below the angle. Referring to the image on the opposite page, if I draw a 2 X 1 angle from the top on March 11, 2014, we find that each subsequent top is a good distance away from this angle. However, if we draw the angle so that it falls more closely to the tops, each top is consistently below the angle and when it does clearly break it, the trend changes.

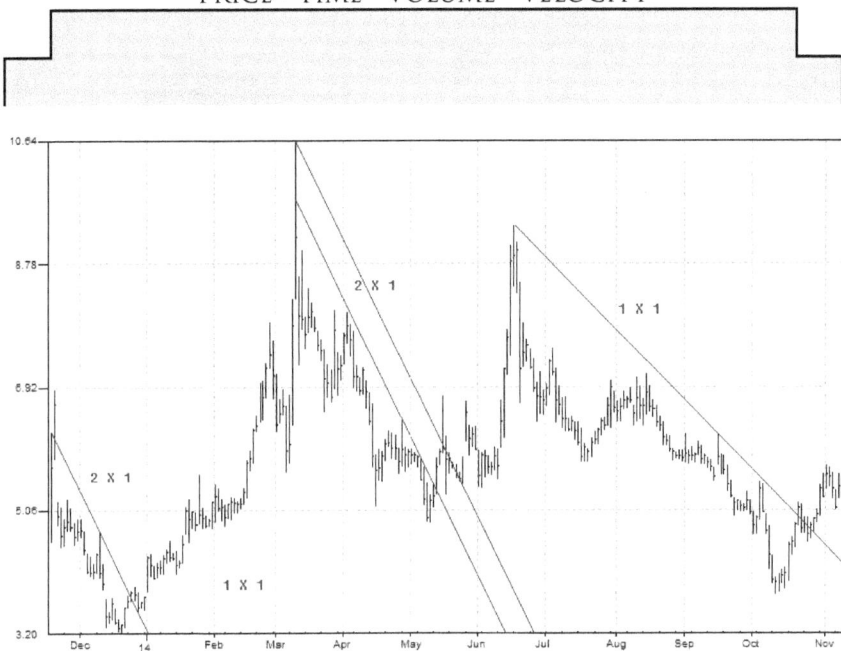

So you can see that instead of drawing the 2 X 1 angle from the November 19, 2013 top, I started it from the top of the previous trading day. This more closely follows the trend down so that when the angle is broken, it gives us an earlier indication of when the trend changes. The same can be said for the 1 X 1 angle from the top on June 17, 2014. Notice that each top is below this angle and when it finally does break this angle, the trend turned up. All of this was based on drawing an angle that closely fit the rate at which the stock was making higher bottoms. For this stock in particular, the rate of 5 cents per trading day worked pretty well for what I was trying to accomplish. That said, another interesting thing worth investigating is squaring price based on the speed we obtained for this stock.

For example, take the high of 689 on November 19, 2013. To calculate how many units of price this value represents, we divide it by our 5 cents. Therefore, 689 divided by 5 is equal to 137.8. Therefore, it would take 138 trading days to square the price. Measuring 138 trading days from November 19, 2013 puts us at June 10, 2014, which is right at the start of the big advance that resulted in the June top.

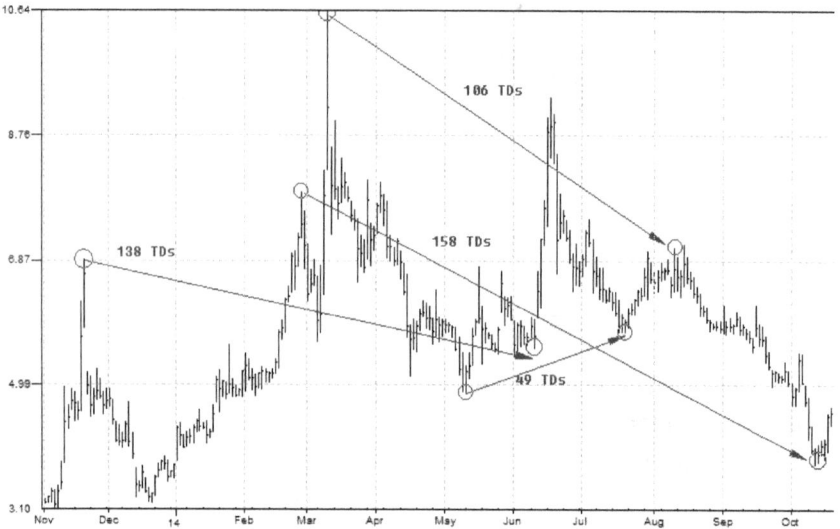

Another point of interest is the minor top of 792 on February 27, 2014. From the low in December to this top, the total volume of shares was equal to the FLOAT during this time. 792 divided by 5 is equal to 158.4. Therefore, it would take 158 trading days to square the price. Measuring 158 trading days from this minor top puts us at October 13, 2014, which is right at the start of the advance.

From the March 11, 2014 top of 1064, we divide by 5 cents and get 212.8. To get the halfway point of this square we divide by 2 and get 106.4. 106 TDs puts you at August 11, 2014 right before the trend turned down. Last but not least, take the low of 487 on May 9, 2014 and divide by 5 cents and you get 97.4. The halfway point of this square is 48.7. 49 trading days from this date would put you at July 21, 2014, which is right before the trend turned up.

We can also square the range and find turning points as well. From November 7 to 19, 2013, the price change was 379. This divided by 5 is 75.8. Measuring 76 trading days from November 19 puts you one trading day past the top of 1064 on March 11, 2014. It is well worth it to play around and see where price turns with respect to these squares and to contemplate why this would be so. Sometimes the change occurs at the end of the squares, at other times the halfway points, and at others at the thirds.

Now, in addition to saying, "When Time is up", Gann also said, "When a Time Cycle is Completed", "Volume Starts" or "Volume Increases". When he uses the words "Time Cycle", I think he is referring to the planetary cycles as described in the early part of this book. This suggests a further relationship with volume and these time cycles. Examples of keeping track of these cycles with respect to the chart can be found in his various courses. I will not go into that in this chapter. The point I wanted to draw out with the past examples is how I believe the angles should be drawn on the chart to coincide with the things Gann said we should expect to see.

Please note, the way the angles worked out on this chart will not work out the same way on every chart. It is my personal opinion that when there is a change in the composition of the outstanding shares or the FLOAT, it affects the scale of the chart and also the angles so that angles drawn from a past low or high may not accurately point out future resistance levels.

5

MATHEMATICAL PREDICTION FORMULA

In chapter three of this book, I made reference to an advertisement from *Forbes* that said,

> *"FORECAST MAJOR MARKET TOPS AND BOTTOMS -dates for TREND CHANGES with the MASTER TIME FACTOR! Only W. D. Gann Research, Inc., offers the Master Time Factor, a mathematical formula for predicting market tops and bottoms . . ."*

The advertisement describes Gann's Master Time Factor as a mathematical formula for predicting market tops and bottoms. I also mentioned that I found this to be of interest because there is a course entitled, *W.D. Gann Mathematical Formula for Market Predictions*, dated September 29, 1953. I wondered if this course contained all the information needed to understand the mathematical formula described as Gann's Master Time Factor. In addition, Gann's promotional booklet entitled, *Why Money is Lost on Commodities and Stocks and How to Make Profits* from 1954 contained a section with the heading, MATHEMATICAL PREDICTION FORMULA.

I also wondered if the material contained in this section provided clues on his mathematical formula. There were four factors listed, which were TIME, PRICE, VOLUME, AND SPEED. In chapter four I showed some places where Gann made references to these four factors and provided some examples on how he used them. In this chapter I would like to go into more detail with respect to the information provided in his promotional booklet on these four factors, and to see what can be learned from the course bearing the words "mathematical formula" in the title.

As stated, in Gann's promotional booklet issued in 1954, there is a section with the heading entitled, MATHEMATICAL PREDICTION FORMULA. Under this section of the booklet it reads as follows:

> *"The four factors: TIME, PRICE, VOLUME, and SPEED have been supplemented by a fifth factor, MASS PRESSURE."*

It is here we learn that in addition to the four factors already discussed, there is a fifth factor that supplements the previous four called MASS PRESSURE. With respect to the first factor listed, which is TIME, it contains the following information.

> *"Time is the essential element. Time cycles which he has developed cover the great time cycle and its important harmonics. Time cycles for stocks, commodities or business can be calculated and projected 100 years or more in advance, subject to minor corrections and variations."*

As we learned in chapter 2, the great time cycle is most likely the 60 year cycle. However, he also refers to another cycle in his *Master Calculator for Weekly Time Periods to Determine the Trend of Stocks and Commodities* as the great cycle. It is also in this course that he also discusses the harmonics of a cycle.

> *"We divide the cycles into 1/2, which is the most important, and also into the periods of 1/8, 1/3 and 2/3, and watch these proportionate parts of the cycles for changes in trend. For example:*
>
> *"The Great Cycle of 90 years equals 1080 months;*
>   *1/2 is 45 years or 540 months*
>   *1/4 is 22-1/2 years or 270 months*
>   *1/8 is 11 1/4 years or 135 months*
>   *1/16 is 5-5/8 years or 67 1/2 months*
>
> *"The 30-year Cycle or any other cycle is divided up in the same way."*

This makes clear the information provided in his promotional booklet under the section on TIME. All cycles are divided up into their harmonics, and when a stock reaches these points it is important to watch for a change in trend.

Continuing on with the information in his promotional booklet, the following is also stated under the section on TIME.

> *"He has proven a TRUE TREND LINE as well as a relatively TRUE TREND LINE when prices are advancing,*

and a relatively TRUE TREND LINE when prices are declining. He has developed rules and indexes which show whether high or low prices will culminate on the true trend line or the relatively true trend line. A time variable and price variable has been worked out to exact mathematical points."

I personally have not came across a direct reference to a TRUE TREND LINE in any of Gann's other courses unless I have overlooked something. I have seen descriptions of a TRUE TREND LINE on the internet, but I am not sure if it is used in the same context as what Gann meant by a TRUE TREND LINE as described in his promotional booklet. All I can say is that it has to be related to VELOCITY. Gann often said that stocks made tops and bottoms at different times, and that it was important to study individual stocks and not averages. Thus, I suspect that the TRUE TREND LINE was something established for individual stocks. I believe that this aspect of TIME has nothing to do with planetary cycles and more to do with the composition of the stock itself.

I must refer back to the quote from the previous chapter that describes this in detail. On page 6 of *Truth of the Stock Tape*, we find the following:

"Market movements depend upon Supply and Demand. It requires volume of trading in proportionate large or small amounts to move stocks up or down. The volume of sales to the stock market is the same as the steam is to the locomotive or the gasoline is to the automobile. The sales are the motive power which drives prices up or down. For example: United States Steel has five million

shares of common stock, and it requires a very large volume of sales to move this stock up or down very much. General Motors has fifty million shares of common stock and its fluctuations are confined to a very narrow range, because the buying or selling of 100,000 shares will not move it more than a point, if that much, while the buying of 100,00 shares of Baldwin will often move it up or down five or ten points, because there are only 200,000 shares of Baldwin outstanding and seldom ever over 100,000 shares of stock floating in the street. Therefore, in order to understand the meaning of volume, you must know the total capital stock outstanding and the floating supply of the stock you are trading in."

So each stock has a different combination of outstanding shares, FLOAT, etc., and this makes the time for each stock to reach top and bottom different.

So to me, there seems to be two different aspects of TIME. One aspect of TIME is related to the stocks outstanding shares and floating supply. The other aspect deals with planetary cycles and their harmonics. It makes sense to me that based on where the stock is with respect to its own composition, it will react differently based on the TIME CYCLE that is coming due. Maybe this is why the repeat of certain TIME CYCLES don't appear to produce the same results. Maybe you have to take both aspects of TIME into consideration. Where is the stock with respect to TIME based on its own individual characteristics?

Moving on, the second factor mentioned in Gann's promotional booklet is PRICE. Under the section on PRICE, we find the following information.

"Mr. Gann has developed rules which show the relation between time and price and what happens when prices complete a cycle before time expires. There is a rule for determining when prices are in balance with time and when prices are out of balance with time. Prices are sometimes behind time and sometimes ahead of time."

In my opinion, the reference to "time expires" is the same as when he says "When Time is up" and "When a Time Cycle is Completed". To add some clarity to the above passage, there is also another section in his promotional booklet worth taking a look at. It is under the heading entitled, 76th Year Trading Record and New Discoveries. It reads as follows:

"In the spring of 1954 he completed a MASTER THREE-DIMENSION CHART which proves the relative position of TIME, PRICE and VOLUME which produces VELOCITY or SPEED and shows when the trend is changing to a very fast active advancing market or a slow upward movement. The relative position of PRICE TO TIME TELLS the TIME CYCLES when prices decline very fast or move very slow. History repeats in the stock or commodity markets but you must learn the rules and the GREAT TIME CYCLES in order to take advantage of rapid advances and declines and make profits."

These two passages highly suggest that the relationship between time and price is of extreme importance. This may be where the squares come into play. In the Mathematical Formula course, they were used to note the relative position of price to time within the square.

Continuing with the section in the promotional booklet under MATHEMATICAL PREDICTION FORMULA, there is more information provided under PRICE.

> *"Rules have been developed showing how long prices and time remain in the transition period. All of the rules prove that TIME is the essential factor and that prices conform to time when a TIME CYCLE is complete."*

I mentioned that it seemed that this is where his squares came into play. More will be said on this later, but my first thoughts after reading this passage was that prices want to go where time is. When you study additional material, it will be essential to keep the above PRICE concepts in mind to see if you can find examples that accurately describe what he is talking about in this section.

The next section under MATHEMATICAL PREDICTION FORMULA is VOLUME. It is very short and to the point and reinforces what has been presented thus far.

> *"Volume is the driving power which moves prices up or down, regardless of whether buying or selling is based on supply and demand or not. The increase in volume increases the velocity of prices in an advancing or declining market."*

With the previous discussion and examples on volume, I think this concept of volume is well understood.

The same can also be said of the last of the four factors, which is SPEED. Under this section it reads,

"Speed or velocity is a movement in price during a unit of time."

This is pretty much the exact definition of velocity discussed in a previous chapter. It is the slope or the angle on a stock chart. It should not be confused with the rate of vibration.

After discussing the four factors, TIME, PRICE, VOLUME, and SPEED, there is a fifth section on MASS PRESSURE, which was a supplement to the previous four. On this it says,

"The fifth factor, mass pressure, shows when the public becomes over optimistic and buys on hope, and after a certain cycle of time, the public becomes pessimistic and sells because they fear prices are going lower. The mass pressure curve can be calculated 100 years or more in the future, as it is subject to only slight variations and minor corrections at fixed time intervals."

In addition to the advertisements and promotional booklet that reference these factors, which are always part of what is described as a mathematical formula, there is also a course bearing the title, *W.D. Gann Mathematical Formula for Market Predictions.*

This course from September 29, 1953 concerns itself with what Gann describes as the Master Mathematical Price Time and Trend Calculator. This was his square plastic overlay. As Gann described it,

"This chart is made on transparent plastic so that you can place it over a daily, weekly or monthly high or low

chart and see at a glance the position on the time and price based on the geometrical angles."

Gann then goes on to describe the components of the plastic overlay.

"The square of 144 is the GREAT SQUARE and works better than any other square both for TIME AND PRICE because it contains all the squares from 1 to 144. This chart is divided up into sections of 9 both for time and price because 9 is the highest digit. Nine spaces on the daily chart equals 9 days, 9 weeks or 9 months in time periods and 9 equals 9¢ on grains, 9 points on stocks or 90 points on cotton on the daily high and low chart. One column in the square of 144 contains 144. This would equal $144 on grain, 144 points stocks or using a scale of 10 points to 1/8 inch it will equal 1440 points on cotton. MASTER 144 SQUARE CONTAINS 324 square inches and each square inch contains 64 units which gives 20,736. This is 20,736 weeks or months and the proportionate parts of this are used for the measurement of time and price because this is the great cycle."

First, there is the GREAT SQUARE, which is the square of 144. There are 144 spaces going across the x-axis and 144 spaces going up the vertical or y-axis. Each space is equivalent to 1/8th of an inch so that every 8 spaces is equal to an inch. If you take the 144 spaces and divide by 8, which is the number of spaces in an inch, you get 18. Therefore, the size of the square is 18 inches by 18 inches. By understanding the size of the square in inches, it helps to understand the statement at the end of the passage where he says the Master 144 square contains 324 square inches. This is because 18 inches times 18 inches is equal to 324 square inches. He also says that each square inch contains 64 units. This is because 144 X 144 is equal to 20,736, and this divided by 324 is 64.

He then goes on to say that the chart is divided up into sections of 9 both for time and price, but goes right into the next sentence saying nine spaces on the daily chart equals 9 days. First, nine sections is equivalent to 16 points as 9 X 16 is equal to 144. So a section on the chart is equal to 16 units of time. Then we must also understand that every space is equal to 1 unit of time, which is why he says nine spaces is equal to 9 days, 9 weeks or 9 months in time period.

The next important fact concerning the square is that you are not limited to 144 days running across the bottom for time or 144 points for price. Even though it is labeled 1 to 144, he gives you an example using a scale of 10 points to 1/8 inch, then it would equal 1440 points on cotton as 10 * 144 is equal to 1440. For NWBO, which I used as an example in the previous chapter, every 1/8 inch was equal to 5 cents. Therefore, if I had a scaled chart for NWBO at 5 cents per trading day, and laid the master calculator over this chart, then the price at the top of the square would be equal to 720 cents, and time equal to 720 trading days.

Now, one of the things that he alludes to is the fact that time is not only measured across the horizontal axis, but it is also tracked within the square itself. Under the section entitled, THE GREAT CYCLE OF THE SQUARE OF 144, he writes,

"The time period of this square is 20,736 days, weeks or months. One-half is 10,368 days. One-fourth is 5,184 days. One-eighth is 2,592. One-sixteenth is 1,296 days. One-thirty-second is 648 days. One-sixty-fourth is 324 calendar or market days. 1/128 is 162 days and 1/256 is 81 days or the square of 9."

This is not a description of time running across the horizontal axis of the square. To explain further, let me use the square of 12 as an example. Just like the square of 144, each space is 1/8 of an inch wide, and it is 12 spaces wide by 12 spaces tall.

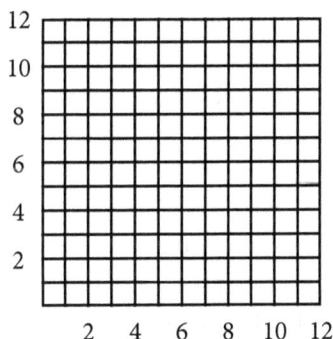

This gives it a total of 144 units or squares. Therefore, the great cycle of the square of 12 is 144 days, weeks or months.

It suggests that time would be tracked through each of the individual squares, possibly similar to how he used the permanent or name chart as described in *W.D. Gann: Divination by Mathematics*. The first day would start at the square in the bottom left corner and proceed up to the top of the square. After day 12, you would go to the bottom of column 2 and this would represent day 13. Going through each of the columns in like fashion, you would reach the end of the square in the top right corner after day 144. So the great cycle of the square of 144 is based on the number of actual square units - 144 X 144 = 20,736. In the course he gives you this time in calendar or market days, then in weekly time periods, and then in monthly time periods.

Under the section of the course with the heading, The Importance of 3 and 5, we find once again the very elements of what we found in the advertisements and in his promotional booklet. It reads as follows:

"The movement in PRICE and TIME whether on a Daily, Weekly or Monthly chart has three important points, the PRICE, the TIME AND VOLUME of sales, the PITCH or TREND which is the geometrical angle which shows whether time is influencing and driving prices up or down on a slow angle or an acute fast moving angle. There are also four factors that influence prices, PRICE, TIME AND VOLUME AND VELOCITY. Time is the most important factor because when time is up volume increases and the velocity or speed of the market increases and the PITCH or TREND on the angles moves up faster or down faster."

The above is followed by a section with the heading, Five Factors for Time and Price. In the last part of this section, there is a curious statement. It reads,

"In connection with the Master Time and Trend Calculator apply all of the rules with the Master Time Factor and geometric angles."

We know that the Master Time and Trend Calculator is the square of 144. We also know that the geometric angles were drawn on the plastic overlay. However, he uses the words "Master Time Factor" as if he has already discussed what it is in the course. Curiously, in the section right before the one being discussed, he talks about the four factors. Once again, I stress the fact that the Master Time Factor was described as a mathematical formula. We also have many references to four main factors associated with what Gann describes as a mathematical formula. The evidence leads me to believe that the Master Time Factor is somehow related to the factors of PRICE, TIME, VOLUME, and VELOCITY and their relationship to each other.

Moving on, he then talks about where you would watch for changes in trend.

"Most changes in trend occur when the TIME PERIODS are at one-half of the square of 144 and at the end of a square or at the 1/3, 2/3, 1/4, and 3/4 points in the square of 144; you must always watch the square in time of the HIGHEST PRICE and the MINOR HIGHS and LOWS, also the square in TIME of the LOWEST PRICE and the SECOND OR THIRD higher bottom, also the time required to square the Range and where the square works out in the Master Square of 144."

So why would most changes in trend occur at the harmonic points of this cycle in particular? Why is this cycle important? Later in the course, Gann writes under the heading, GREAT YEARLY TIME CYCLE:

"To pass through the square of 144, which equals 20,736, it requires 56 years, 9 months and 23 days, which is a very important time cycle. Next in importance is 1/2 of this time period which is 28 years, 5 months and 8 days and 1/4 which is 14 years, 2 months and 19 days. The 14 year cycle is always very important because it is 2 seven year periods. 14 years equals 168 months and 169 months is the square of 13 making it very important for a change in trend and this is also an important time resistance point. 1/8 of the Great Cycle is 7 years, 1 month and 10 days and is quite important. 1/16 is 42 months and 20 days, 1/32 is 21 months and 10 days. This is an important time period because it is close to 22-1/2 months which is 1/16 of the circle of 360 degrees."

What seems the most obvious explanation as to why this cycle is important is that its harmonics are very close to the square of certain numbers or close to the harmonics of a circle. Yet, I don't understand why these squares would be more important than any others.

So far in this book, we have seen examples where Gann identifies the Great Cycle as a cycle of 60 years, a cycle of 90 years, and now a cycle of approximately 57 years. More importantly, this latter cycle is connected to the course bearing the words "Mathematical Formula" in the title, which we can tie to his Master Time Factor. Needless to say, this cycle is also worthy of further investigation.

The square of 144 is a period of 20,736 days, which is approximately 56.77 years in length. What is odd is that it doesn't seem to correlate with any obvious planetary cycles. Yet, this time period is very close to 56 years, which is a well known cycle identified in many things. In fact, it is very close to the 55.8 year cycle of the lunar nodes, which consists of three nodal cycles of approximately 18.6 years each. Even though the time period in the Great Cycle is approximately one year greater than 55.8 years, I contemplated the possibility that this is the true cause of the cycle within the Master Calculator.

If you take 55.8 years and multiply by 365.24219 days you get 20,380.514202. If you take the square root of this number you get 142.76. Is it possible that Gann simply rounded up to 144 because of its ease of use due to the fact that so many numbers can factor into it? Is it possible that this could also serve as a means of hiding the cause of the cycle within the Master Calculator? Although I am only theorizing, there is more evidence to support the 55.8 year cycle and its role in the Master Calculator.

The moon's nodes are the points at which it transitions from South to North across the ecliptic and from North to South across the ecliptic during its monthly cycle. When crossing from South to North, the moon is said to be at its North Node. When crossing from North to South, it is said to be at the South Node. The nodes are always in opposite signs in the zodiac, and they take approximately 18.6 years traveling backwards through the signs to complete a cycle.

What I find interesting is the fact that one of the key harmonics of the Great Cycle described by Gann was its division into thirds. Each third would then correlate with 18.6 years of time. The other reason why it seems important is the fact that Gann's financial timetable is based on the same cycle. On the following page I have re-created Gann's financial time table.

FINANCIAL TIME TABLE

compiled by W.D. Gann (1909)

1784	1803	1821	1840	1858	1877	1895	1914	1932	1951	1969	1988	LEGEND
1785A	1804A	1822A	1841A	1859A	1878A	1896A	1915A	1933A	1952A	1970A	1989A	A - Extreme low stock prices, strikes, repression, despair, beginning of new business generation of 18.6 years. 4 years of rising stock prices and improving business. Markets bare of goods, Young men becoming prominent.
1786	1805	1823	1842	1860	1879	1897	1916	1934	1953	1971	1990	
1787	1806	1824	1843	1861	1880	1898	1917	1935	1954	1972	1991	
1788	1807	1825	1844	1862	1881	1899	1918	1936	1955	1973	1992	
1789B	1808B	1826B	1845B	1863B	1882B	1900B	1919B	1937B	1956B	1974B	1993B	B - High stock prices.
1790	1809	1827	1846	1864	1883	1901	1920	1938	1957	1975	1994	
1791C	1810C	1828C	1847C	1865C	1884C	1902C	1921C	1939C	1958C	1976C	1995C	C - Panic.
1792D	1811D	1829D	1848D	1866D	1885D	1903D	1922D	1940D	1959D	1977D	1996D	D - Low stock prices.
1793	1812	1830	1849	1867	1886	1904	1923	1941	1960	1978	1997	
1794	1813E	1831	1850E	1868	1887E	1905	1924E	1942	1961E	1979	1998E	E - High stock prices.
1795E	1814F	1832E	1851F	1869E	1888F	1906E	1925F	1943E	1962F	1980E	1999F	F - Panic.
1796F	1815	1833F	1852	1870F	1889	1907F	1926	1944F	1963	1981F	2000	
1797G	1816G	1834G	1853G	1871G	1890C	1908C	1927G	1945G	1964G	1982C	2001G	G - Low stock prices.
1798	1817H	1835	1854H	1872	1891H	1909	1928H	1946	1965H	1983	2002H	H - Very high stock prices, most prosperous year, waste over-extravagance, most money in circulation, much speculation.
1799H	1818	1836H	1855	1873H	1892	1910H	1929	1947H	1966	1984H	2003	
1800J	1819J	1837J	1856J	1874J	1893J	1911J	1930J	1948J	1967J	1985J	2004J	J - Major panic - CRASH! 4 years of falling prices, business stagnated, breadlines, soup kitchens, despair, unemployment.
1801	1820	1838	1857	1875	1894	1912	1931	1949	1968	1986	2005	
1802	1821	1839	1858	1876	1895	1913	1932	1950	1969	1987	2006	
1803	1822K	1840	1859K	1877	1896K	1914	1933K	1951	1970K	1988	2007K	K - Same as A plus strikes, unemployment, many prominent deaths.
1804K	1823	1841K	1860	1878K	1897	1915K	1934	1952K	1971	1989K	2008	
		1842										

Dec. 25, 1989 revises to Mar. 13, 1934.

Notice at the top that it says it was compiled by W.D. Gann in 1909. Also notice in the legend under "A", the reference to the 18.6 year cycle. Starting with the year 1784 at the top, the year in the next column is calculated by adding 19 years to 1784, which is 1803 at the top of column two. To the year in column two, 18 years is added to get 1821. This alternation of adding 19 then 18 years continues across the top of the table. This averages out to 18.5 years, but we know the nodal cycle averages about 18.6 years in length. Therefore, at some point in the process a correction has to be implemented to keep the years and the position of the lunar nodes in sequence.

The comment on the bottom right of the table says that December 25, 1989 revises to March 13, 1934. This is a direct reference to three nodal cycles, which is approximately 55.8 years. There are exactly 20,376 days between these two dates, which is 55.78764 years. If we cast a geocentric chart for these two dates, which is shown on following page, we find that the nodes in 1989 are not in the exact same position as they were in 1934.

Before proceeding any further, I have to clarify that there are two ways of calculating the position of the nodes. One is mean node, which is an average, and true node takes into account the non-uniform motion of the nodes where although its main direction is retrograde or backwards through the zodiac, there are times when they do go direct. So there is a slight difference in the position of the nodes based on which one is used. After looking at both, I can't say for sure why Gann said December 25, 1989 revised to March 13, 1934. Using mean node, it is 1° behind its 1934 position. Using true node it is about 2° beyond.

I would have thought that the dates would show the nodes in the exact same positions. I even looked for additional planetary relationships as to why he chose this date in 1989, but nothing stood out. For the chart below, the nodes are mean nodes.

Inner Wheel
Transits Mar 13 1934
Event Chart
Mar 13 1934, Tue
11:47 am EST +5:00
New York, NY
40°N42'51" 074°W00'23"
Geocentric
Tropical
0° Aries
Mean Node

Outer Wheel
Transits Dec 25 1989
Event Chart
Dec 25 1989, Mon
7:49 pm EST +5:00
New York, NY
40°N42'51" 074°W00'23"
Geocentric
Tropical
0° Aries
Mean Node

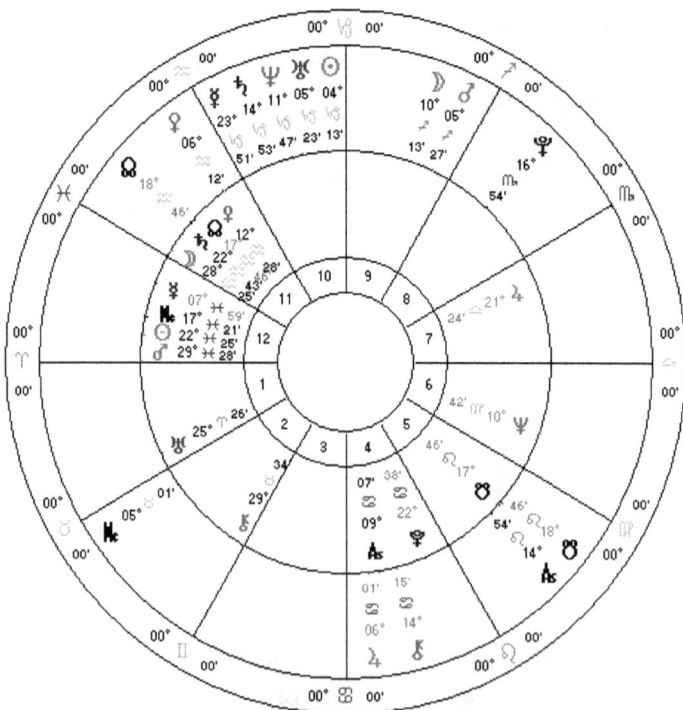

One of the things I did notice was that the angles between the Sun and Moon on both dates were relatively the same, so I adjusted the time on those dates to make the angular relationship the same, which is 24° in both instances. On January 24, 1990 around 6:34 p.m., the nodes would be within 35 seconds of conjunction and the Sun and Moon in the same angular relationship. So to me, the January date would make more sense if the angular relationship was important. The same can be said if using True Node where an earlier November date would make more sense if the angles between Sun and Moon were important.

In addition to the obvious reference to the period of 55.8 years in the table, and the fact that this period consists of 3 nodal cycles of 18.6 years each, the cycle itself also contains some interesting dynamics that are worth noting. Back in the days when I started studying cycles, I was part of a cycles group that granted members access to archives of Cycles Magazine. There were a lot of interesting articles that I read during those times, and one of the many that I printed and saved, (which was hard to do), was written by David McMinn entitled, *The Sun, the Moon, and the Number 56*. In the article he writes,

> *"Every 56 years, the sun conjuncts (0° angle) the moon's north node in almost the same zodiacal position (3° clockwise) and on the same date (minus three or four days). Every 56 solar years (or 59 eclipse years), the sun's relative position is approximately the same angle to the north node, with the moon 180° on the opposite side of the zodiac."*

Using our date of March 13, 1934 from Gann's financial time table as a starting point, lets see what McMinn was talking about by looking at the chart below.

Inner Wheel
Transits Mar 13 1934
Event Chart
Mar 13 1934, Tue
11:47 am EST +5:00
New York, NY
40°N42'51" 074°W00'23"
Geocentric
Tropical
0° Aries
True Node

Outer Wheel
Transits Mar 9 1990
Event Chart
Mar 9 1990, Fri
11:47 am EST +5:00
New York, NY
40°N42'51" 074°W00'23"
Geocentric
Tropical
0° Aries
True Node

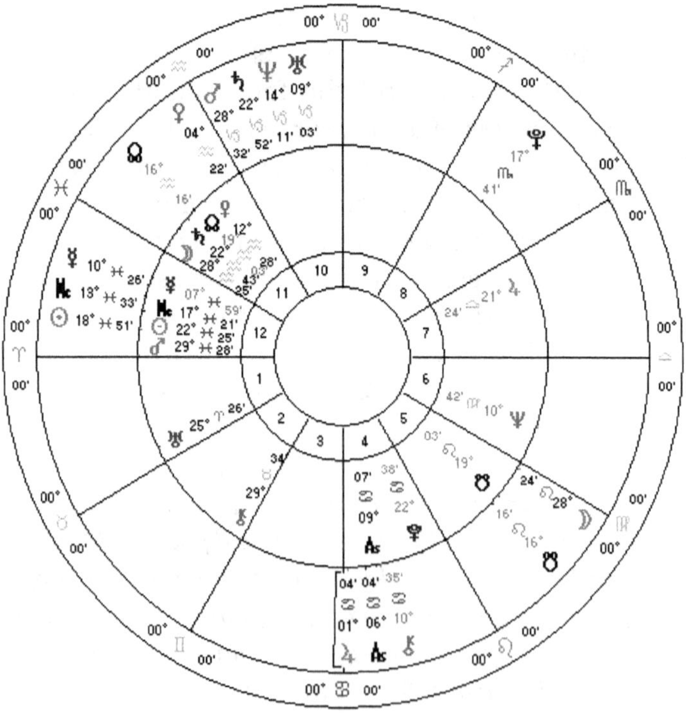

First, notice that in the inner wheel, the angle between the Sun and North Node is approximately 33°. Likewise, in the outer wheel the angle is also approximately 33°. The moon in the inner wheel is at 28° Aquarius and in the outer wheel it is at 28° Leo in the opposite sign.

So Gann's financial time table has at its foundation, the nodal cycle of 18.6 years. It says it was compiled by Gann in 1909 so we know he had it at the beginning of his career. If you go through the table it is remarkable how accurate the legend is with respect to the years in question. Yet, there is no trace of Gann mentioning the nodal cycle or the 56-year cycle in any of his subsequent courses after 1909. It is only in the 1950s that we find a possible reference to the importance of this time period through the Master Calculator.

When Gann used the term "Great Cycle" prior to the 1950s, we know that he was referring to a cycle of 60 years. He talks about this cycle and its harmonics as being important. Yet, in the 1950s when he says "Great Cycle", he is talking about a cycle of 90 or approximately 56.77 years. As I mentioned before, the time period of the nodal cycle and its harmonics have been found in many things. In one of my notebooks from 2009, I wrote down some facts concerning this very cycle.

The notes centered around the fact that drought and rainy weather is connected to the nodal cycle of 18.6 years. Part of the notes were based on an article written by Louis M. Thompson entitled, *The 18.6-Year Lunar Cycle: Its Possible Relation to Agriculture*. Louis M. Thompson also wrote another article in the May/June 1989 edition of Cycles Magazine entitled, *The 18.6-Year Cycle in the General Economy*. In this article Thompson writes,

"About 20 years ago I ran across an unusual chart in Harlan Stetson's book, Sunspots in Action. The chart had been prepared before 1885, and it predicted the business cycles to the year 2000 with surprising accuracy."

This chart from the article is shown below. Notice that the panic years coincide with the section of years corresponding to the letter "J" in Gann's financial time table. In addition, the years 1854, 1872, and 1891 labeled BOOMS, also correspond nicely with letter "H" described as years of very high stock prices in Gann's time table. Likewise, the BOOM years 1827, 1845, 1864, etc., also correspond nicely with letter "B" described as high stock prices in Gann's table.

A CHART FOUND MORE THAN 100 YEARS AGO - 1885

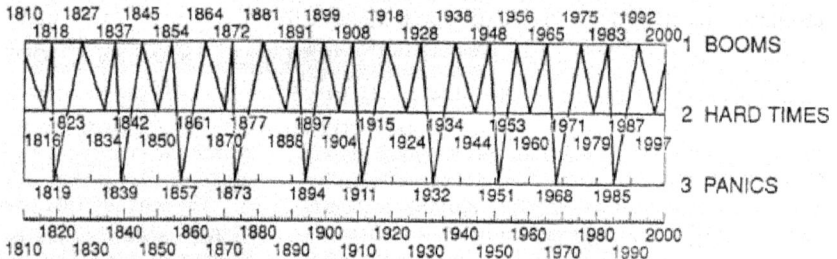

FIG. 1. Chart published in Dun's Review in 1937. The numbers 1, 2, and 3 on the Y axis probably referred to footnotes in an earlier version.

The article says that this chart used to hang over the desk of a certified public accountant by the name of Charles Hecht, and that it had been found in an old distillery in 1885. As Thompson points out in the article, the nodal cycle is a lunar declination cycle.

There are four key points in the lunar declination cycle. When the North Ascending Node is near the equinoctial point or 0° Aries of Western charts, the moon can reach a maximum declination of 28.5° in the Northern Hemisphere. When the North Ascending Node is near the equinoctial point or 0° Libra, the moon can have a declination of only 18.5°, which is the time of minimum declination in the Northern Hemisphere. The other two points occur when the North Node is near 0° Cancer and 0° Capricorn when the declination of the moon is equivalent to the tilt of the earth to the plane of the ecliptic, which is 23.5°. These are the midpoints of the lunar declination cycle. Thompson also provides us with a graphic of this cycle with respect to the general economy, which is shown below.

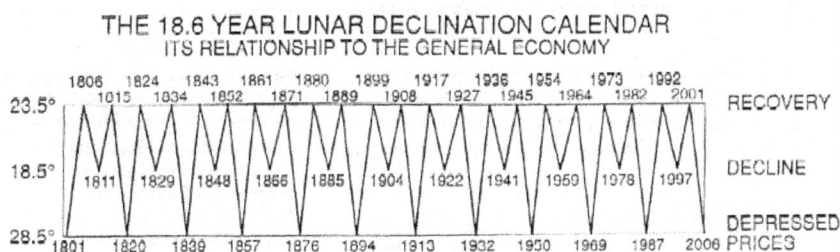

THE 18.6 YEAR LUNAR DECLINATION CALENDAR
ITS RELATIONSHIP TO THE GENERAL ECONOMY

Compare the chart above to Gann's financial timetable where 1927 is labeled "G", which indicates low stock prices. It is followed by two years of high stock prices, but 1930 begins the period labeled "Major Panic - Crash, from 1930 to 1932. After 1932, we have a period of rising stock prices and improving business conditions. This is from 1933 to 1936. Then from 1937 to 1938 high stock prices. On page 83 of Tunnel, we find the following:

"Another bad period for the United States will be 1940 to 1944."

In the table, 1939 is labeled Panic and then low stock prices in 1940, 1941, and 1942. 1943 is labeled high stock prices, but is immediately followed by a panic in 1944. So according to the table, 1940 - 1944 is indeed characterized mostly by low stock prices and panic, which could be the very reason why he wrote what he did.

As you read Gann's books and materials, I would encourage you to take the time to note how he describes the times, and compare it to his financial table. For example, on page 2 of Tunnel we also have the following:

"Capt. Gordon was a farmer, growing mostly cotton crops on the Red River bottom lands. The following year, 1907, after the birth of little Robert, Capt. Gordon's crops were almost a failure. The Spring was late and overflows damaged cotton. This, together with unfavorable financial conditions, caused a panic in the United States in the Fall of 1907."

Now, look at the financial table and you see 1907 is labeled "F", which stands for panic.

The other thing that is worth noting with respect to Gann's financial timetable is the fact that certain events in the legend seem to repeat in periods not in uniform with the nodal cycle. For example, take the high stock prices of 1919 and there are also high stock prices in 1924, which is 5 years later. Even though high stock prices repeat every 18.6 years, the other highs are do not repeat at harmonic intervals such as the halfway point of the 18.6 year cycle. What I noticed is that if you take the Great Cycle of the square of 144, which is 56.77 years, and note the halfway point, it is a little over 28 years. Gann said it was an important point to watch for a change in trend. If you start at 1919 in the Financial Table and add 28 years, you get 1947, which is also another year of high stock prices. Add 28 to 1947 and you get 1975, which also falls under high stock prices. Therefore, high stock prices will repeat every 28 years. So 28 years would be a nodal cycle plus another half cycle of 9.3 years, which would put the nodes in opposite sides of the zodiac, meaning that eclipses will still occur in the same earthly seasons. 27.9 years or the halfway point is $1.5 * 18.6$. Since 27.9 is a little less than 28 years, you would have to adjust for this by subtracting a year after a certain amount of time.

Gann also mentioned that 1/4 of the Great Cycle was important, which is 14 years. Not surprisingly, Gann's Financial Timetable also seems to embed a 14 year cycle. Starting at 1947 it is labelled "H" for very high stock prices. Add 14 years and we get 1961, which is labelled "E" for high stock prices. Add another 14 years and we get 1975. This is one year more than 1974 which is labelled "B" High stock prices. After the third cycle of 14 years from 1947, there is a break in the pattern where 1975 + 14 is 1989, which is labelled "K" and "A" for extreme low stock prices. Then adding another 14 years and you are back on the pattern.

It is also worth mentioning that a 60 year cycle is also embedded in this table. For example, start in 1810 labeled "C" Panic and add 60 years and you get 1870, which is labeled "F" Panic. Add another 60 years and you get 1930, which is labeled "J", which is described as a major panic.

Adding another 60 years you get to 1989/1990, which is labeled "A", described as low stock prices. This appears to be a break in the pattern, but a minor adjustment to the starting year, and adding another 60 years puts you back on the pattern again.

Not wanting to get too far off subject, we see that the Great Cycle of the square of 144 appears close to the 55.8 year cycle, which is three nodal cycles of 18.6 years each. Recall that the master calculator is also divided into nine sections. Therefore, if using the nodal cycle of 55.8 years, each section is equivalent to 6.2 years, which is also a well known cycle found in many things. Last but not least, dividing 55.8 years into 8 sections, we get the 7 year cycle or 6.975 years. So maybe the Great Cycle of the square is working out these natural time periods, which are in actuality, related to the nodal cycle.

The last thing I wanted to mention is that the description of Gann's Mass Pressure Chart seems very familiar to the panic and booms of his financial time table. Recall that his Mass Pressure chart is said to show when the public becomes over optimistic and buys on hope, and after a certain cycle of time, the public becomes pessimistic and sells because they fear prices are going lower. This could very well be the Panics, Low Stock Prices, and High Stock Prices of his Financial Timetable.

There is much more in the course entitled, *W.D. Gann Mathematical Formula for Market Predictions*. More clarity is still needed with respect to the relationship between Time and Price and what Gann meant by a cycle of Time versus a cycle of Prices. With respect to these topics, I have provided the quote from page 92 of this book below for convenience.

In his promotional booklet under the heading entitled, 76th Year Trading Record and New Discoveries. It reads as follows:

> *"In the spring of 1954 he completed a MASTER THREE-DIMENSION CHART which proves the relative position of TIME, PRICE and VOLUME which produces VELOCITY or SPEED and shows when the trend is changing to a very fast active advancing market or a slow upward movement. The relative position of PRICE TO TIME TELLS the TIME CYCLES when prices decline very fast or move very slow."*

Gann says that the relative position of TIME to PRICE tells the TIME CYCLES when prices decline very fast or move very slow. In other words, the relative position of TIME to PRICE influences VOLUME because as we learned, an increase or decrease in VOLUME is what causes a corresponding change in VELOCITY, and an increase in VELOCITY is what causes prices to move up or down faster. As I briefly mentioned before, Gann related TIME to PRICE through the use of his squares and wheels. On page 92 of this book I also provided a quote from Gann's promotional booklet from the section under PRICE, which I am providing below for convenience.

> *"Mr. Gann has developed rules which show the relation between time and price and what happens when prices complete a cycle before time expires. There is a rule for determining when prices are in balance with time and when prices are out of balance with time. Prices are sometimes behind time and sometimes ahead of time."*

I think this provides a clue as to what to look for when working with his squares or wheels. The relative position of PRICE to TIME within one of these squares should show us a corresponding change in VOLUME. Knowing what to look for may be helpful in properly scaling the chart given that if the relative position of TIME and PRICE are the same, VOLUME should respond in the same manner also.

Unfortunately, after going through the various courses that explain how to use the Master Calculator, I did not find an example that illustrates the relationship between TIME and PRICE in this manner. The examples provided tell a different story. It provides you information on the current position on angles from prior highs and lows, and you judge the trend for the current time period accordingly. In my honest opinion, this doesn't have anything to do with the relationship between TIME and PRICE as he described it in his promotional booklet. I find it hard to believe that his true mathematical prediction formula is simply noting the time from previous highs and lows and the current position of price with respect to the angles and resistance levels of the master calculator from these highs and lows. Maybe the true mathematical relationship between these factors is the Master Time Factor.

Since Gann stated the importance of knowing the relationship between PRICE, TIME, VOLUME, and VELOCITY, my goal in this book was to take a closer look at the relationship between these factors to better understand what Gann may have meant when referring to them. It is my sincere hope that something in these pages has assisted someone with their own research, and will stimulate others on to further research. Peace & Blessings.

~

BIBLIOGRAPHY

Awodele, *W.D. Gann: Divination By Mathematics*, Union, KY: BEKH, LLC, 2013. Print.

Awodele, *W.D. Gann: Divination By Mathematics: Harmonic Analysis*, Union, KY: BEKH, LLC, 2013. Print.

Azad, Kalid, "An Interactive Guide to the Fourier Transform" *Better Explained*. Date article published not available. Accessed September 29, 2015. http://betterexplained. com/articles/an-interactive-guide-to-the-fourier-trans form/.

Chang, Pao L. "Frequency, Vibration and Oscillation - The Energy Patterns That Affect Your Wellbeing" *Waking Times*. June 10, 2014. http://www.wakingtimes.com/2014/06/10/ frequency-vibration-oscillation-energy-patterns-affect-well being/.

"EquiVolume" *StockCharts*. http://stockcharts.com/school/doku. php?id=chart_school:chart_analysis:equivolume.

"Forecast Major Market Tops and Bottoms - dates for Trend Changes with the Master Time Factor!" *Forbes Incorporated*. 1952. Page 32. https://books.google.com/ books?id=tTNEAAAAIAAJ&q=%22only+w.+d.+gann+ research%22&dq=%22only+w.+d.+gann+research%22&hl =en&sa=X&ved=0ahUKEwishu-IiPrKAhXBnIMKHZutD poQ6AEIJTAA.

"Frequency and Period of a Wave" The Physics Classroom. http:// www.physicsclassroom.com/class/waves/Lesson-2/ Frequency-and-Period-of-a-Wave.

Gann, W.D., *Master Calculator for Weekly Time Periods to Determine the Trend of Stocks and Commodities*. January 10, 1955.

Gann, W.D., *Master Time Factor and Forecasting by Mathematical Rules*. November 1935.

Gann, W.D., *Method For Forecasting the Stock Market*. January 1931.

Gann, W.D., "Sees the Kaiser Shot While Trying to Fee His Prison." *The Milwaukee Sentinel Magazine*. 5 January 1919.

Gann, W.D., *The Tunnel Thru the Air Or Looking Back From 1940*. New York: Financial Guardian Publishing Co., 1927.

Gann, William D., *Truth of the Stock Tape: A Study of the Stock and Commodity Markets With Charts and Rules for Successful Trading and Investing.* New York: Financial Guardian Publishing Co., 1923.

Gann, William D., *Wall Street Stock Selector: A Review of the Stock Market With Charts, Rules and Methods for Selecting Stocks.* New York: Financial Guardian Publishing Co., 1930.

Gann, W.D., *W.D. Gann Mathematical Formula for Market Predictions.* September 29, 1953.

Gann, W.D., *Why Money is Lost on Commodities and Stocks and How to Make Profits.* Pomeroy, WA: Lambert-Gann Publishing Company, 1954.

Letters by W.D. Gann to John H. Spohn and Dr. John De Jonge. Gann Study Group. https://groups.yahoo.com/neo/groups/gannstudygroup/info.

McMinn, David, "The Sun, the Moon and the Number 56." *Cycles.* Vol. 46, No. 4, 1997: 99 -103. Print.

Moore, Henry Ludwell, *Economic Cycles: Their Law and Cause.* The Macmillan Company., 1914.

Newlands, John A. R., *On the Discovery of the Periodic Law, and On Relations Among the Atomic Weights.* New York: E. & F. N. Spon, 1884.

"Newton's Second Law" The Physics Classroom. http://www.physicsclassroom.com/class/newtlaws/Lesson-3/Newtons-Second-Law.

"Open Season for Prophets Is On: What 1922 has in Store for Us May Be Forecast Until Jan. 1." *The Sun.* 28 December 1921.

Smithson, James, "Rediscovering Gann's Law of Vibration" *Trader's Journal.* 21 October 2008.

The Seeker, *My Story - The Search for W.D. Gann's Master Time Factor.* 1983.

Thompson, Louis, "The 18.6-Year Cycle in the General Economy" *Cycles.* May/June 1989: 139 - 141. Print.

Thompson, Louis, "The 18.6-Year Lunar Cycle: Its Possible Relation to Agriculture" *Cycles.* March/April 1989: 65 - 69. Print.

"Types of Forces" The Physics Classroom. http://www.physicsclassroom.com/class/newtlaws/Lesson-2/Types-of-Forces.

W.D. Gann on the Law of Vibration. Gann Study Group. https://groups.yahoo.com/neo/groups/gannstudygroup/info.

W.D. Gann on The Master Time Factor. Gann Study Group.
https://groups.yahoo.com/neo/groups/gannstudygroup/
info.

Who was OROLO?. Gann Study Group. https://groups.yahoo.
com/neo/groups/gannstudygroup/info.

"William Gann - A Legend" *Future Analyzer: Dharmik Market
Timing.* Date article published not available. Accessed in
2015. http://www.futureanalyzer.com/education/william-
gann-legend/.

Weston, Professor, *Forecasting the New York Stock Market.*
Pomeroy, WA: Lambert-Gann Publishing Company, Inc.,
1986.

Wyckoff, Richard D., "William D. Gann: An Operator Whose
Science and Ability Place Him in the Front Rank - His Re-
markable Predictions and Trading Record." *The Ticker and
Investment Digest,* Vol. 5, No. 2. December, 1909: 51-55.

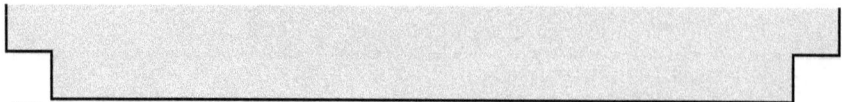

ALSO AVAILABLE FROM THE AUTHOR

W.D. GANN: DIVINATION BY MATHEMATICS

W.D. GANN: DIVINATION BY MATHEMATICS: HARMONIC ANALYSIS

OBSERVATIONS ON W.D. GANN VOL. 1: PERIODICITY

THE ORDER OF PLANETS IN VIMSHOTTARI DASHA

www.ingramcontent.com/pod-product-compliance
Lightning Source LLC
Chambersburg PA
CBHW070408200326
41518CB00011B/2108